THAT THEY MIGHT HAVE JOY

THAT THEY MIGHT HAVE JOY

COMPILED BY:

PHILLIP R. KUNZ, GAIL W. PETERSON, EVAN TYE PETERSON

ISBN: 1-55517-262-8

1 2 3 4 5 6 7 8 9 10

Published and Distributed by:

CFI

Cedar Fort, Incorporated
925 North Main, Springville, Ut 84663 801-489-4084

Cover Design by Lyle Mortimer
Page Layout and Design by Rene Muñoz and Tosha Baker

Printed in the United States of America

Table of Contents

INTRODUCTION

What brings joy into our lives, especially in times of trouble and distress? What increases our joy in times of happiness and fulfillment? Perhaps you have asked yourself these questions or perhaps you have had moments when you needed a reminder of better times. Truly, as the scriptures tell us, "Men are, that they might have joy. (2 Nephi 2: 2 5.)

In our day, many of our brothers and sisters, some in and some out of the Church, are experiencing events in their lives that might lead them to forget the promise of those words "that they might have joy." Knowing this, we contacted members of the Church throughout the world to ask them, "What has brought you some of your greatest joys in belonging to the Church?"

It took several years for us to gather the material found in this book-material from good people from four years of age to over ninety, people who have found moments of joy in the small everyday experiences of living, and people who have known great moments of spiritual manifestations. These experiences, great and small, typify the joy that many of us have in this life and through the gospel.

From hundreds of responses to our questionnaires, responses from every walk of life and many foreign countries, we found ourselves almost overwhelmed by the honest love and concern we found in others, a desire to share "the good news." Yet, we were ever reminded that to many these were sacred experiences and difficult to share. Many cautioned us to remember the sanctity of

spiritual experiences and asked that their names be with-
held, though they wanted to share their joy in the gospel
with others. We have, therefore, changed our original
intent of giving names and backgrounds and have instead
presented simple descriptions of the fine brothers and sisters represented here. We hope that we have done justice
to them all.

We hope that as you read these beautiful experiences
that you will feel the love and hope that they so warmly
present. We hope these experiences of joy and sorrow will
be helpful as you prepare talks, face trials, and/or need
thought stimulation. We hope, too, that you will find
new friends—brothers and sisters in the gospel who have
shared their stories in this collection.

In closing these prefatory thoughts, may we share one
more scripture with you, a scripture referred to by a
young woman who has found much "solace and comfort
and inspiration" in the scriptures.

> Therefore, let us glory, yea, we will glory in the Lord; yea,
> we will rejoice, for our joy is full; yea, we will praise our God
> forever. Behold who can glory too much in the Lord ? Yea,
> who can say too much of his great power, and of his mercy,
> and of his longsuffering towards the children of men? Behold,
> I say unto you, I cannot say the smallest part which I feel.
> (Alma 26:16.)

That is how we feel. We know, from reading hundreds
of responses, that this is the way members of the Church
throughout the world feel as well. We hope that as you
enjoy and use the book, that you will find joy in sharing it
with others.

A Mother's Love

There was a long period in my life when I was very ill. My children were small and sometimes I wondered if I would live to raise them. They were so very precious to me that I could hardly bear this thought. I and lived very close to my Father in Heaven at this time. I pleaded for his help and that I might have the blessing of raising my family. My mother had passed away before any of my children were born. She was such a wonderful mother, so kind and good and comforting when we were sick as children, and I felt the need for her strength and love so badly during this difficult time that I prayed for her help and asked my Father to let her help me and be near me. This prayer was answered, though I had never anticipated that it would be. The experience I had is as real to me today as it was that night when I was sitting halfway up in my bed.

It was 1:00 am. I could not sleep because I was so miserable. I looked over at the other bed in my room where one of my four children was sleeping. Tears ran down my cheeks as I thought about my children and my love and concern for them. Just then I felt a personage from the world of spirits come into my room. This person was standing by my bed. I said: "What do you want?" Then this person leaned over me and I felt the warmth of my mother. Her spirit conveyed the tenderest love, sympathy, and comfort one could ever imagine.

Though she left my room after a short while, I could never deny that she came.

I do believe that spirits return to earth to give comfort and assurance or counsel to loved ones. I know as a mother that if there way any way I could, I would return to comfort my children when they needed me. After this experience, I had the feeling that I would get well, and gradually I did. I have enjoyed the privilege and blessing of raising my family. I am now doing genealogy on my mother's line.

A Father's Love

Although I had been raised in the Church and had always been active and believed with all my heart that the gospel was true, I secretly longed for that special assurance wherein I could say, "I know." Soon after my marriage, in the early morning hours as I was in my dairy barn milking my cows and thinking of serious things, an extremely penetrating voice came to me. I know not if it was audible or just for me alone, but it said, "You know. You know!" It penetrated to the fiber of my heart and soul. My greatest desire had been granted and I *did know*!

Some twenty-five years later in the same setting— my dear wife's birthday, I received another spiritual experience. I was sorely in need of comfort and strength to carry on. Three months to the day earlier, we had lost a good, fine son in Vietnam- a son who had filled an honorable mission, graduated from college, married a wonderful girl in the temple who was soon to have their child. The sorrow and heartbreak we had all experienced was indescribable.

This special morning I was thinking of our much loved son, and it seemed that the veil became very thin. I could actually feel his presence there in that milk house where we'd spent so many hours together in his younger years. His message to me that morning was one of love—an expression of the deep love he felt for all of us—his parents, his wife, and infant son, his brother, his sisters, his grandmothers and other relatives, and his friends. A marvelous feeling of warmth, assurance, gratitude, and renewed testimony of God's eternal plan enveloped me and gave me the strength I needed on that special day.

Life After Death

I have always known the Church to be true, but there are some things we believe that are hard to comprehend, like life after death. I had an experience that proved to me that this principle is true. When I was about twelve years old, my great-grandmother died. I went with my father to her funeral in Idaho. When we got there and went to see her body, relatives wanted me to touch her hand. Of course, I was frightened. I could imagine touching her and having her sit up and smile at me. So most of the time that I was there, I stayed as far from her as I could. Just before the casket closed, I touched her cold hand, then just stared at her.

For many nights after that I could not sleep. Then one night I dreamed she came to me and told me there was no reason to be frightened and that she was alive. Since then I have never been afraid or doubted that there was life after death.

Rarotonga

While serving a mission in the Rarotongan Mission in the South Pacific (our mission included the set of thirteen islands in the Cook Island network), I was asked to travel with and translate for President S. Dilworth Young. I was to be his counselor and translator for the three weeks he visited our mission.

One Sunday afternoon I was translating a talk he was giving in a district conference. He would speak for two or three minutes and then I would translate into Maori. I was really feeling good about the entire situation until he opened his Doctrine and Covenants and started reading. The D&C, at that time, had not been translated into the Maori language, but he would read about three sentences and then I would translate them. This continued for a while back and forth. Every once in awhile he would stop to give an example or explain a certain point.

Once right in the middle of my translating, he stopped me and said: "Elder, are you sure you translated the right number?" For a minute, I stopped, and sure enough I was wrong. The funny thing about this is that the numbers in Maori cannot be understood unless you know Maori very well or have someone tell you. Since President Young didn't speak Maori, it was obvious he was told the right number through inspiration.

Then, he continued to read from the D&C. I had never heard the passage he was reading and the meaning was not clear to my mind. I remember my mind going blank. The next thing I remembered, President Young was sitting beside me saying, "Elder, I lost you up there, didn't I? That's OK, because when the weakness of man comes in the way of the Lord's work, the Lord takes over in his own way."

I could not quite figure out what had happened. All I knew was that one minute my mind went blank and the next minute the talk was over. Missionaries and members were coming up to tell me what a great job I had done translating his talk, but I still didn't understand what had happened during the time my mind went blank.

Two days later, President Young and I were traveling to another branch when he began to explain to me for the first time what had really happened. When I was standing there with a blank mind, the Holy Ghost took over to finish the talk for me. Then and there I gained a testimony of great strength of how the Holy Ghost works.

Experiences such as this and the ones the Lord has in store for the future help us to realize the joy the gospel can bring into our lives. It is my testimony that we are without a doubt children of our Father in Heaven and that he lives and answers our prayers if we will but listen and take heed of his words.

Love, Don

On Friday, November 14, 1958, my husband, a career Air Force officer, and seven other men bailed out of a crippled C119. The carburetor heat door regulator had failed and caused the engine to ice up. They were returning to Hill Air Force Base, Utah.

The day after the bailout (Saturday), the bishop came to visit and see how we were doing. I had such good feelings about this wonderful bishop. I sat down very close to him and searched his face. I inquired of him pleadingly, "Is my husband alive?" He said, "Yes, he is." I said, "You are telling me in your official capacity as the bishop that he is still alive?" He repeated, "Yes, he is." I said, "If you are telling me this, I know he is alive."

During the next week, the bishop spent every spare minute he had with us. My four children soon loved him as much as I did. Many nonmember or non-Mormon Air Force friends came in to help me and the bishop made quite an impact on their lives. They loved him.

The next Saturday morning I again inquired of the bishop, "Is my husband alive?" He replied, "It's in the hands of the Lord." I said, "Then I know he's dead."

My husband's body (the last to be found) was frozen after ten days in the bitter Utah winter and was returned to Hill Air Force Base Hospital. An autopsy confirmed that he had died on Saturday evening, November 15, 1958. He had written me a note at 0700, November 15: "Lena, I love you and the kids. Take good care of each other. Love, Don."

The Witness

I was lying on my bed listening to General Conference over the radio. It had been one of those sleepy Sundays and I was only half aware of the words being spoken. I sort of became conscious that President Lee was closing the conference with his talk but not much of it was registering even then. Suddenly I sat up and it was like an electric current running through me. My mind and spirit tuned into every word the Prophet was saying. I knew at that moment that this man was truly God's mouthpiece, and that he was speaking the words of Christ. Perhaps I have forgotten the details of his talk, but I will never forget the witness that came, the Spirit that seemed to come right into the room from the radio. This knowledge has brought me much joy in knowing that we *are led* by an inspired man of God, and that through following his counsel we will never go astray.

In the Presence of a Prophet

My wife and I were privileged, along with over 23,000 others, to attend a Brigham Young University devotional at which President Harold B. Lee, prophet, seer and revelator of the Lord, presented an address. We arrived at the Marriott Center at nine o'clock, one hour before the address by the Prophet was to begin. Already thousands of students had arrived, but we were able to locate a good seat. I tried to busy myself by reading various books, but was unable to concentrate on even the scriptures as we waited for President Lee's arrival.

I sensed very strongly the great feeling of expectancy as the huge crowd awaited his entry. I had been privileged to meet the President on two former occasions. The first occurred in the assembly room of the Salt Lake temple. After attending two endowment sessions (for many of us, our first experience inside a temple), over three hundred

young missionaries were to have the opportunity of ques-
tioning Harold B. Lee, then first counselor in the First
Presidency, concerning temple endowment procedures.
At that time I was impressed greatly by President Lee's
command of the scriptures, as he answered our questions,
often quoting verbatim from the Doctrine and Covenants.

These thoughts helped the time pass more quickly
until President Lee, accompanied by his wife, entered the
Marriott Center. The atmosphere, already highly charged
by the expectant waiting of such a large audience, was
fairly alive with emotion as we stood as one and began
spontaneously to sing, "We Thank Thee, O God, For A
Prophet." Tears appeared at the corners of my wife's eyes
and rolled down her cheeks as she saw the prophet for the
first time. I, too, was unable to sing because of a throb-
bing ache in my throat.

President Lee did not disappoint us. The tears in my
wife's eyes and the ache in my throat did not subside as a
Prophet of the living God spoke to us for close to an hour.
The Spirit bore witness to us, with a sweet, powerful
influence that cannot be denied, that the man before us
spoke the truth; indeed, at that time, he was speaking the
words of the Lord Himself.

As we left the assembly we chose not to speak, but
rather to reflect upon the message; but more than that,
upon the effect the mere presence of a prophet had upon
us.

The Mia Maid

One of the most choice and happy experiences in the Church came while I was a Mia Maid teacher. All summer I had anticipated almost with a feeling of reluctance, my new class of Mia Maids. There were so many girls in the class with problems of one kind or another. One of the girls especially concerned me. Her mother and father were divorced and before she had really adjusted to the divorce, her mother died and her father remarried. I knew that her life was at a real turning point.

The night of our first class arrived. I gave each girl a card and asked her to state her HONEST reason for being at MIA. After the class, as I read the cards, my fears were realized as I came to this girl's card and read, "I'm here to see if you are like all the rest - *cold* in a friendly way." The next week she returned, and the next, and the next still giving me a chance but still holding back.

During November, as we were planning our class Christmas party, I felt strongly impressed to ask her to decorate our room for the party (incidentally, something we'd never bothered to do before for just a class party) and from then on she bloomed. The excitement, the work and the effort she put into it was beautiful. Week after week, during the next one and a half years that she was in my class, I watched with a grateful heart her growth in the gospel. Even though she moved from the area, we have remained in touch. What a thrill to be with her this past summer when she took out her endowments in the Provo Temple prior to her marriage in the Arizona Temple to a choice Elder!

A Prayer

This story was related to me by my grandmother, It
took place at Idaho in her early married life. She had five
children at the time and three of them were primary age,
with the oldest being eight years old. She sent them to
primary, which was three miles from their home. While
they were gone, a terrible wind came up with hurricane
force which carried parts of buildings and anything in its
path considerable distance and then dropped them to the
ground shattered to pieces. she watched the hurricane
pick up an incubator we had in the yard and carry it some
distance and then dash it to the ground. She was concerned for the three girls at primary. To get home, they
would have to cross a bridge over a canal and she feared
the wind would pick them up and drown them in the
canal. She was also fearful to leave the two she had at
home, not knowing if the house would withstand the
wind. After some thought, she decided to put the two
small children in the cellar where they would be safe, and
go to find the girls. It was hard to make any headway
because the wind wouldn't permit her to stand very long
at a time. She had managed to walk and crawl about a
mile to a bend in the road which was still on their side of
the canal. As she looked up, she could see her three girls
walking down the middle of the road with no apparent
effort. As she approached them, she came into a calm
area that surrounded the girls and as long as she was close
to them, the wind didn't effect her.

She asked the girls if they weren't afraid to venture
home from primary in the wind storm. They said yes,
that the wind had started blowing when they were about

half way home and they remembered being taught that if you prayed, everything would be okay. So they knelt down by the fence and prayed for Heavenly Father to protect them and watch over them. They were able to walk on home, protected by the calm, where they found the house still standing and the other two children scared, but safe.

The RH Factor

My husband and I had what was called the RH factor, one parent having positive blood and the other having negative. After our first twins were born, the doctor informed us that we may not be able to have any more children because of this factor. My husband and I decided to try and have another child because we both so desperately wanted one. In September, 1949, I gave birth to a little boy. In those days doctors knew little of this RH problem and did not know how to care for our child because he was born with positive blood. In the hospital, he got a high fever that was so bad it burned his nervous system out. Mike was like a vegetable that neither moved nor crawled. He would just lie and cry day and night. He lived for nine months. I knew the night Mike died because I had a dream in which I saw him walking toward heaven as a full-grown man. I awoke and went in and found him dead.

For several months after that I tried to persuade my husband to have another child, but the doctor had convinced my husband of the dangers to my health. One night I had a wonderful dream in which the Lord's angel came to me and told me not to be troubled or worried, that I could go ahead and have children and the Lord would bless me with this joy. Nine months later, I gave birth to a little girl. She had negative blood and was able to live and grow healthy. My next four children were all born with negative blood and healthy. My last little girl was born with positive blood, but a serum had been invented to protect her. This is only one of my joys of having the gospel, but the dearest one to my soul. The Lord does indeed answer prayers.

To My Son

I'm writing this for my son. Ryan was born nine weeks premature weighing only 3 lbs., 14 oz. at birth. The doctors were concerned and told us it would be touch and-go for about a week. He was so tiny, needed constant attention, and constant oxygen to survive.

It was only a few hours after his birth that my husband and our bishop gave him a blessing. When my husband walked in the door after the blessing, all fears about our son melted away. I never doubted after that moment that he would live. I knew that he had a purpose for being born and would live to fulfill that purpose.

He has been a special blessing in our home, and has brought us great joy. I'm grateful for the priesthood in our home, for the meaning it gives to our existence.

A Special Blessing

I had been married for four years. Many doctors had examined me and found nothing wrong, yet no babies came to our home. I received a special blessing by Elder Matthew Cowley. Ten months later, our first son was born. We have since had six more children.

Like a Song in Your Heart

One of my greatest joys in the gospel is that of singing hymns. I have always really enjoyed singing and especially when it's gospel oriented. I have one experience that strengthened my love for singing Church songs and the knowledge that the Spirit of God will be with you.

I had taken my roommates to my hometown for the weekend and on the way back it had started snowing. When it got dark, we were in a canyon and the roads were covered with snow. All the way we had been singing— first we sang all different kinds of songs, then Primary songs and then hymns. While the others were singing, I had noticed my car lights were getting dim. I started worrying about them and finally they went completely out. The moon was bright and with the snow I could see the roads enough to stay on. I was afraid to stop because we were out in the middle of nowhere and also I just had a feeling to keep going. When my roommates quit singing, I told them to sing some more. I had such a feeling of reassurance when they sang—a feeling of peace, that everything would be all right. Half the time it was as if I wasn't even driving the car. I know someone was watching over us because we made it okay. I'll never forget that experience.

To me the gospel is like a song in your heart. I'm thankful for things like that to help me feel the power of God.

The Youth of Zion

January was the date set for the stake south conference. It was to be a snow trip to Big Bear Mountain. The youth were looking forward to this with great expectations. As advisers in the APYWMIA program, my husband and I were asked to be chaperons. Because of work responsibilities, my husband could not attend. So leaving my children with grandparents, I went with the youth.

Thursday morning, January 3, we gathered at the stake center with sleeping bags, suit cases, duffel bags, inner tubes, and even two or three pairs of skits. The youth were hopeful. There had been no snow in the mountains for a month. Though they continued to pray for snow, as of that morning, there was still no snow reported.

After packing the buses, trucks, and a few cars up with our 225 youth, many leaders and assorted paraphernalia, we were off to the mountains.

As we neared the tops of the mountains, the prayers of the youth were answered. Snow was falling softly all around the buses. We cheered and thanked our Heavenly Father. The youth knew all the time that He would answer their prayers.

Excitement grew as we anticipated the next few days with snow. (The youth leaders had even planned volleyball and basketball outdoors just in case.) As we finally got everything out of the truck, buses, and cars into the hall of the camp we had borrowed, our leaders informed us that the youth response was so great that the camp would not be able to house all of us. It was decided that the Laurels and Priests were to go to camps or cabins a mile away and be bussed in the mornings and back at nights. That night we enjoyed a get-acquainted dance.

A bus took the first year Laurels, another adviser, and me to our cabin. We unpacked, claimed our spaces, looked around and prepared for bed.

The next morning we awoke to find our doorways half-blocked by snow. The snow hadn't stopped since we came up the mountain. We knew that there wouldn't be a bus to get us, so we got ready and started to walk to camp for breakfast and activities. The stragglers got a ride.

This was to be our last evening in the mountains. The special speakers arrived around dinner time and the evening of entertainment and special talks was a building occasion for many. That night, though, we were told that we were snowed in. The crews were trying to clear roads but the snow never stopped. They were letting traffic down, but none could come up. We had one bus and our several cars all buried under at least a foot of snow. Reactions were mixed.

The next morning the girls in our cabin dragged and carried as much as they could back to camp in waist deep snow. There wasn't going to be any coming back. Saturday activities continued as outlined. Testimony meeting was one of tears. Girls and boys shed tears of love and appreciation for family, friends, and advisers. A non-member boy working at the camp bore his testimony and wept also. Promises were made that meeting attendance would increase. Youth vowed to start getting up early and attending seminary. They vowed to treat brothers and sisters better. They knew that the Church was true and especially that Heavenly Father existed, answered their prayers, and would answer our prayers now for protection.

We found an L.D.S. family living next to the camp that housed the Laurel group. Because of the storm, there was now no traffic up or down the mountains. No one knew when the storm would subside and how long we would be snowed in. Fresh foods were not getting through. Store supplies were fast diminishing as people realized what might happen. The Red Cross was trying to evacuate our camp and another camp of youth stranded many miles away.

At our camp, we tightened our belts and the next day was one of the finest fast Sundays. With all of us and our families and friends at home fasting and praying, there was never a closer group.

Relief Society and Priesthood were held before Sunday School. There were lessons and speakers. Sacrament meeting was exactly that—a meeting for the purpose of partaking of the sacrament. I have never seen the sacrament administered or partaken of with more reverence for the Lord and His Son than it was that day. Dinner that evening was much appreciated. That Sabbath was one of the holiest I've seen. We were one.

The next morning it was announced that there may be a chance of our one bus getting down. But no one knew when another would be getting back. It was decided that the first year Mia Maids would leave first and the others would stay. The boys helped to dig out the bus and shovel the snow off the buildings.

Finally, the snow plows reached our camp. We were able to get the bus and one car out of about four feet of snow. Leaving behind our friends, brothers and sisters, and those we had grown to love so much was a trial. There were many, many tears shed. Brothers and sisters were never closer.

All the way down the mountain, we sang hymns. We sang every hymn in the book and many from the Junior Sunday School book. Imagine teenagers wanting only to sing hymns.

At the foot of the mountain we passed our three other busses waiting to get back up. At least we knew they were close. We cheered when we saw one of our chapels. We arrived home with only what we could carry, wet, cold, and filled with love. The others came down the mountain safely the next day.

No one can tell me there is no hope for the youth of this world. The youth of Zion will not falter. I know Heavenly Father chose well when he chose these special spirits for the last. I've enjoyed working with them and the children of Zion wherever they live.

Early Text of the Book of Mormon

I am not a good writer of compositions, and I find that it is difficult for me to put my thoughts down on paper. It does, though, give me an opportunity to consider the many blessings the Lord has given me. By far the most important thing to me is my sweet wife and three wonderful sons. The teachings of the Church make it clear that we can be a family unit forever. The kids are really a lot of fun and it is exciting to see how easily they learn and accept the teachings of the Church.

Recently one of the most exciting experiences that I have been privileged to have relates to the Book of Mormon. In doing research on the early text of the Book of Mormon, I have spent hour after hour—day after day— in a careful study of the original manuscript located in Salt Lake City. Many times I have felt almost like I was sitting in on Joseph Smith as he dictated line after line to Oliver Cowdery, the scribe. It is thrilling to see how the text flows on and on without a single mark of punctuation or deletion to change the direction of the story. The Book of Mormon is true and was written by inspiration from God. I never cease to marvel at the great storehouse of wisdom contained in that book.

The Lord is truly blessing me far beyond my worthiness and obedience. I am thankful for the opportunity given to make improvements and re-dedicate myself for greater service.

The Struggle for Self-Worth

I grew up in an LDS home where our parents taught us correct principles and lived lives usually exemplifying those principles. As I passed through my teen years, events happened and situations came about that clouded my perspective concerning my worth as a person. In comparing myself with others, I felt that something was lacking in me. I did not have as pleasing a personality as others. I was not as pretty. I was afraid to interact with people for fear of failure and being laughed at. I told myself over and over that there must be something wrong with me. In order to increase my self-esteem, because I felt so lacking socially, I withdrew from social situations and began to feel self-righteous—like I was better than those with whom I could not compete on other levels. I also let the good grades I got in school place me, in my mind, above others who did not consider good grades so important.

As I went away to college, I took with me all these feelings. To compound these negative feelings, I also took with me feelings of bitterness and self blame for some failings which I discovered in my parents. I had placed them on pedestals most of my life and when I realized they were human and made mistakes, they fell hard. I was directly involved in one of these mistakes and very bitterly blamed myself, my father, and my mother. Because of this experience I also decided that I must be very much different from other people—I must be somehow abnormal.

As my years at college progressed, the realization gradually came to me that I was self-righteous and that I did not love people as I knew I should. I was very unhappy. I came home each evening after working and going to school, hating people. This made me feel even worse about myself. I trusted hardly anyone and thought no one could like me as a person. I had no one I felt I could talk to or confide in.

As I started to understand my true character—that I was not better than everyone else and that I really didn't like myself—my feelings started building up so that I could not concentrate on school work and one night I remember being so sick of spirit that I was physically ill. I really did not want to live although I knew suicide was not the answer.

The only thing I could think to do was turn to the Lord in prayer. I had an experience earlier that year while studying for my Book of Mormon class that testified to me that Christ really loved–in the most pure sense of the word–those Nephites whom he had visited. With this testimony and with the hope that he might love me, too, and forgive me, I got down on my knees and told him with all honesty that I felt love for no one, not even myself. I said I knew this was wrong, that I desired to change, but could not do so on my own. I asked for his forgiveness and his help–and I asked that I might forgive others, especially my parents. Then I asked him to help me learn to love and respect myself.

That was the beginning of a long hard road toward gaining a proper perspective of myself and others. Along the way, I have experienced other situations against which I have had to struggle to come closer to obtaining a feeling of self-worth. Because of these experiences, I have come to begin to understand that joy comes from within, not from how other people think of us or treat us. It comes from within as we try to keep the commandments, as we repent when we have failed, and as we forgive those who have caused us hurt and grief. It comes from a knowledge within that Christ loves us each individually and that we must learn to love each other likewise. The greatest joy that has come to me as a member of the Church is the realization that in the eyes of my Father in heaven, I am a person of much worth.

The Book of Mormon

After almost a lifetime of study of the Book of Mormon, I am still astounded by its relevance, its depth, its universality, its appeal, its structure. I move from pedestrian composition to poetry of high beauty, from simplicity to profoundness and complexity, from straightforward narrative to intricate arrangement. I am enthralled by its variety in characterization, its wealth of incident, its originality.

The doctrine is generally clear, often deep, frequently shattering in its implications. As literature, it does not yet approach the Bible though it has an appeal of its own, a genius peculiar to itself. As history, it is still obscure. As to geography, it is as controversial as it ever was. It is a striking combination of humanity and divinity. The divinity overwhelms me; the humanity delights me.

I could convince the Supreme Court of the United States that no man nor group of men in our time prepared it. Its teachings are too broad and deep, its prayers too penetrating, its totality too convincing, its claims too pervasive.

In Subtle Ways

There is, I think, no greater joy in life than that joy which comes from doing what one knows to be right. It is not necessary to be visited by angels or shaken by earthquakes in order to come to a realization of the might and goodness of our Lord. Just as good things may come in small packages, so too can good and great things come in subtle ways.

In 1972, I drove with four missionary elders from Farmington, Maine, to Augusta, the state capitol, and was there baptized and confirmed a member of The Church of Jesus Christ of Latter-day Saints. There were no blaring trumpets. A new star did not appear in the heavens. Yet I was filled with joy, knowing that I had taken the steps my Father in Heaven would have me take.

When my first poems were published, and later, when my first collection of poems came into print, I felt a great sense of accomplishment. Still, no feelings of pride could compare with the subtle, warm feeling of having been baptized into the Lord's Church, of having done the right thing.

Church Membership

I married a man who was not a member of the Church. His complete conversion to the gospel three months after our marriage and its implications in our present and eternal life stand out in my mind as the major event of my life.

Jim had investigated the gospel for three years and had been rather active in Church for a year and yet still had an agnostic's view of God and life. It was not until he received an inspired challenge from our mission president ("fast and pray until you know, one way or the other") that things began to change .

We went through a difficult three day period of fasting and prayer (in the middle of an illness). Finally Jim decided there was too much he couldn't explain and the stakes were too great to chuck the whole thing, so he requested baptism. This meant a total and sudden commitment to all aspects of the gospel of which he was aware and a determination to know that which he didn't then know or understand.

The implications have been far-reaching in our lives. My husband and I have held Church positions since the week of his baptism. We are expecting our ninth child in nine and one-half years of marriage. This right to inspiration has determined our job and living situation, sometimes in spite of the advice of loving friends and relatives. To me the unity of our commitment is the incomparable benefit of Church membership. It has sustained us through the death of our infant daughter and mental retardation of another. I would not trade this unity of eternal perspective for anything in this world or another.

That Mormon Look

My conversion took place four years ago while I was trying to work out my life and looking into everything except religion. One of the ways I tried to find something better was through drugs—I was deeply involved for over four years. This proved to cause nothing but more problems for me, however. After about three and one-half years my body started rejecting almost every drug I put into it. I decided then that someone was trying to tell me something, so I started backing out of the drug scene slowly. It was hard because all my friends were drug users. I, being a weak person in some ways, couldn't turn off immediately to things I was used to doing for so long.

I went to visit my best friend one night (who by the way was into drugs) and upon arriving at her home I immediately noticed something different about her but I couldn't put my finger on it. I hadn't seen her for some time so I thought maybe she had changed her hair style. When I asked her about it, she told me she needed to talk to me. I spent the next two hours listening to her testimony. I have never felt so close to the Lord in all my life. The Holy Ghost bore witness to me that day that the Church was true. That day I found out that a boy I admired and respected very much was a Mormon, so my girlfriend and I decided to go over and tell him I was going to investigate the Church. When we arrived at his house and told him, he looked at me really seriously and said, "I've been waiting for you to say that." He told me he wanted to tell me about the Church for a long time, but he knew I wouldn't listen because I wasn't yet ready. He also told me that he knew four years ago that I would join because I had that Mormon look. Well, six months later I was baptized.

A Stake Mission

One night our bishop visited my husband and me and asked us if we would fill a stake mission together. My immediate reaction was to say no. My children were still in high school, I worked full time as a secretary, and I had a large home with a beautiful yard and swimming pool to keep up. Since my husband worked at both a full-time job and a part-time job and on the side played in a dance band one or two nights a week in order to pay for our gracious way of life, I couldn't expect much help from him at home. Besides, I already had a job in Church; I led the singing at MIA. My husband held about six positions at once. We didn't need to go on a stake mission.

And so I was about to respond to our bishop with an emphatic no when I glimpsed at my husband's face and knew that if I did, his spirit would curl up and die. His answer to the bishop was yes for himself, but he couldn't speak for me. I stalled the bishop until the next day and went to bed. The look on my husband's face haunted me.

My question to the bishop the next morning on the telephone was, "If I accept this calling just to make my husband happy and from no desire on my part to go on a mission, is that a good enough reason?" Fully expecting a negative answer along with a sermon, I was almost crestfallen by his response: "If you go on this mission, you will convert yourself." I had no recourse. I accepted the call.

That morning before I left for work, realizing how really little I knew about the gospel, knowing that when I became a missionary, investigators would expect me to be a source of religious knowledge and a paragon of virtue, I began to quake; and I picked up the scriptures, searching for something that would comfort me. As I read (and I don't recall the specific scriptures I read), I was amazed to feel my heart swelling and tears warming my eyes. I couldn't wait to get home from my office that evening to read more scriptures. Night after night I sat up, reading until I could stay awake no longer—the standard works, *Jesus the Christ, The Articles of Faith.* The scriptures and the gospel had become "delicious to me." I had been born again.

I can testify that the godly power which comes through one small act of unselfishness can transform an individual's life. I didn't work for it; I hadn't been steadfast; I didn't deserve it. But it happened to me.

From Doubt to Certainty

Doubt. That's a big word you know. Especially when you have been doing what you think is right for fourteen years and then all of a sudden it hits you, "I don't really know for sure." That's what happened to me. Brought up in the Church, baptized at eight, active in all Church activities and then all of a sudden I thought, "Is the Church really true? How can I be sure there is a God? How can I be sure that what other people believe isn't true?" I remembered that my teachers in Church had said that I'd have to find out for myself one of these days, but I had thought that I knew. Well, I decided to find out. I was a little bit scared because I wasn't sure whether there was a God, and if there wasn't, then the Church would be false, and that kind of upset me.

One night I was awake for a long time, just thinking. I lay there looking at the stars through my window and finally said, "If there is a God up there, please let me know." And then I decided that even though I wasn't sure about God that I'd pray until I found out for sure. If I got that conviction people said they got about the Church from praying about it, then I'd know for sure it was true. But if no answer was forthcoming then there must be something else of truth in this life. About one week later, I was still in deep thought about this. I had fasted once and prayed continuously that I would have some answer. On the way home from school I found myself on the bus alone, which was very unusual, for the bus usually had loads of kids I knew on it. Anyhow, I said another silent prayer and then the most beautiful little voice just seemed to tell me that there was a God, that He loved us, that I was doing good and right, and that the Church was true. All those things swept over my mind, completely from another power other than my own, and I felt comfort and peace in my heart and soul. My eyes filled with tears and I realized that I, at last, had my answer. I thought, "This is real joy—to feel so peaceful and warm and good, and to know that my Heavenly Father loves me, and that he cares enough to answer my prayers."

Oui, Monsieur

A wood stove warmed the small kitchen. His gold rings reflected in the yellow light. Frere J. rolled his faded denim work sleeves past his elbows, rested one arm on the table, and with the other stocky hand pulled at his long white sideburns while I looked through his dented tobacco can stuffed with worn snapshots. I came to his forty-year-old wedding portrait.

"She was very beautiful," I said, "I'm sure you loved her very much."

"Very much, monsieur." His blue eyes glistened.

"In this picture when you were married, it was until death do you part." He pensively fingered the snapshot. "She's dead now."

"You're not married any more?"

"She died seven years ago," he said softly.

"Would you like to live with her again?"

He shrugged his shoulders. "Oui," he muttered.

"Jesus Christ came to the earth," I began, "and gave authority to his apostles that what they sealed on earth would be sealed in heaven—even marriage could last through death. That authority is on the earth; I know it is. You can live with your wife again if you do as I tell you. Do you want that?"

Frere J. looked at the portrait, then steadily at me, bewildered at such a strange, wonderful proposition. He sat slowly back, then firmly replied, "Oui, monsieur."

An Experience in France

Some of the experiences which have brought the greatest joy into my life are sacred in detail, but can be summed and reviewed nonetheless. Certainly one of the greatest joys is the exhilaration that comes in sharing successfully the message of the restored gospel. I think in particular of an experience in France, when a young girl whose soul was filled with bitterness, pessimism, and distrust, came to know the brotherhood of the Church and the sweetness of the spirit.

She was a friend of an investigator who had received all of the discussions but lacked parental permission to be baptized. This good investigator introduced M. to the missionaries who made friends with her and began to teach her the lessons. Upon receiving the fourth lesson on physical and spiritual death, M. began to cry, left the room, and decided not to see the missionaries again. Several months later, my companion and I ran into her and began to reteach the six discussions. She explained that a year previous her sister had died in an operation when a doctor had made a mistake. M. felt that no one, not her family, nor her sister's husband, nor the doctor, nor the priest cared at all about her sister's death. She withdrew within herself, learning to distrust all people, hating close human contact, and denying God. We worked carefully with her challenging her at every step to seek God in humble prayer. She finally really reached the point at which she needed to know—not having faith, but desiring honestly to find out.

After I was transferred, her prayers were answered at a mission-wide youth conference. One of the greatest joys I have known was to receive word that this young woman had been transformed into a kind, loving, devoted, and enthusiastic Saint. She was baptized in the ocean in September, 1972, marking in some way the extent to which her life had been renovated, Similar experiences in home teaching and in personal friendships have borne out the conviction I hold that to share the gospel's glad and joyous tidings is one way that we experience true joy.

My Father's Death

One interesting event I'd like to relate concerns the preparation I had as well as my whole family had in the passing of my father. He was taken in mid-December.

The previous summer our family enjoyed the first reunion where our whole family was able to get together for the first time since before my sisters and brothers started marrying. My oldest sister felt impressed to begin a discussion about obtaining grave plots for our parents. Both my parents were quite set back, yet realized the importance of her message and plans were made. However, no real effort was put forth afterwards until it had to be done. I continued in school that fall and one night truly suffered an evil nightmare. When I awoke, I was sitting up straight in bed and I had aroused my brother in the next bed. It left me with a feeling I have never forgotten. After that I had a thought running through my mind very often. It was, "What are you going to do when you father's gone?" This was unconsciously sitting at the edge of reality and I really didn't see it until its full impact suddenly startled me at his funeral. This shell of mine really felt empty then.

My father was on the high council until a month before his death. He often commented that he didn't know why he was released, an interesting note to ponder.

I know I haven't felt the true joy that can yet be encountered. I hopefully look forward to that exquisite event, the continuous joy of being with our Lord. I express to him gratitude for all He has given me. This has been a good experience for me to review my many blessings. I hold these things special and sacred and they constitute part of the basis of my faith and my life.

Heartache

I believe that one of the greatest spiritual experiences that I ever had was at the time in my life when a tragedy occurred. Shortly after returning from my mission, my younger sister and her husband were killed in an automobile accident. I had never felt such a heartache in all my life. As time passed and through prayer, I was able to come to an understanding that it was not my position to judge, and I should understand that their situation was and is in the hands of our Father in heaven. Since that time, I have felt many times the influence of my sister and her husband. The incident actually strengthened my faith and the faith of my family.

The Doctor's Recommended Amputation

There have been many occasions in my life where faith and prayers have effected healing with my family and with myself. As a small child, I can remember being told of a beautiful example of faith exhibited by my dear grandmother at the time my own mother lay helpless in bed as a result of a car accident. At the age of fifteen, she faced losing her leg because of the injuries. The doctors recommended amputation. Her doctor told my grandmother that there was no hope of saving the leg. Imagine the sorrow for a beautiful young girl who loved to dance more than anything.

My grandmother called the elders in to administer to her daughter and the spirit of faith filled the room. The Lord's hand effected a dramatic improvement so much so that when the doctors arrived the next morning to perform the operation, they were amazed and proclaimed it a miracle that the leg was improved, at least to a point that they could work to save it.

At the age of 74, my mother still enjoys dancing and meets once each week with friends to participate in Senior Citizen's activities.

A Special Prayer

Several years ago we were vacationing at our cabins in the Stanley Basin. My father had pulled a tree down for the use of firewood and in the process hurt his back and could only walk with great difficulty. At times, he would pass out. We were thirteen miles away from the nearest town and nearly eighty miles from the nearest doctor and the car would not start. My parents had always been active members of the Church and because there was no other priesthood holder among us Mother put her hands on my father's head and said a special prayer that all might be well. She then took my brother who was about six and, leaving my older sister, myself, my two younger brothers and my father, walked about seven miles until she and my brother were picked up and driven into town. Through her faith, my mother soon secured help and we were able to get Dad home and to a doctor. He is now all right. This is only one of the many experiences that I have enjoyed because of the gospel.

The Lord's Loving Protection

When I was eighteen, our family was in a serious car accident. I was driving. Our car was hit from the left rear while we were going about 65 miles per hour. The impact was great and our car left the freeway, went over an embankment, over a gully, through a fence, and onto another road and finally stopped. Observers told us our car went high into the air. We should have rolled over. We should have all been killed. My mother was five months pregnant. She lost her four front teeth, but not the baby.

I look back on the experience now and I know the Lord carried our car to safety. I did not panic after we were hit. I sat at the wheel calmly. Dirt covered the windshield so I could not see, but I held the wheel steady and did not slam on the brakes.

This was a miracle in our family. I know the Lord
lives. I know He protects his children. Our car was
totalled, but out of the seven in the car, only my mother
was hurt. We are all grateful for the Lord's loving protection over our family.

Temple Marriage

One of the greatest joys which I have in belonging to
the Church of Jesus Christ of Latter-day Saints is that of
being blessed with a temple marriage. I remember the day
vividly as though it happened yesterday. On the morning
of December 14, 1973, my future wife and I drove down
Parley's Canyon on the way to the Salt Lake Temple. The
canyon was covered in white, shining snow. Everything
was so quiet and peaceful. When we arrived, the morning
air was crisp and cool. As we were ushered into the temple by smiling workers, I had such a strange feeling in my
stomach, one of excitement and anticipation. We went
through a session, which seemed to set the stage for the
wonderful act to be performed.

We were then showed into a marriage room which
was so beautiful. Mirrors reflected our images without
end; the Spirit of the Lord was there. The light in the
room and the light radiating from those present seemed
to be different from any other light known to man.

As I looked across to my mate and looked into her

eyes, I could not hold back the tears for I knew she would be mine forever and ever.

At the Side of My Weeping Mother

At the time of the passing of President George Albert Smith, we lived in a small converted granary which we called home. As I recall there were then four members of our family in addition to Mother and Father. Our means were sufficient and we enjoyed the blessing of a love-filled home.

My awareness of this incident comes to life with the usual household tasks occurring. I remember that my mother was preparing food of some sort. The radio was on—a small brown RCA—which brought a goodly amount of static along with its spoken word and music.

All of a sudden, a strange hush fell over the house and Mother spoke in soft tones almost a whisper. "We must continue our work quietly," she told us. "President Smith's funeral is being broadcast."

I recall not a word that was spoken or sung at that service, but I do recall that in a matter of moments I noticed that my mother was weeping quietly.

Why did my mother cry? She had never met this man. I had never seen her cry before. I must know why this thing was making my mother sad.

I went to her. I looked up into her face. The tears streamed down her cheeks. Not a word was spoken but I knew that Mother knew something very special about President George Albert Smith. I vowed within my young

heart that I would be good enough to someday know
what it was.

With the passing of each prophet since that time,
beginning with President David O. McKay, I have wept
unashamedly as the Spirit bore anew that testimony
gained at the side of my weeping mother.

A Precious Loan

Unable to have a family, we applied to LDS Social
Services for a child and after nineteen months of waiting
we received our son the day before Thanksgiving. Then a
grueling year of anxious waiting passed until final adoption. One week after this adoption, we took our son to
the Provo temple to be sealed to us.

It was the Friday before Christmas and what a beautiful and special day, what a fitting way to celebrate the
birth of our Savior. I shall never forget the peace and joy
that filled my heart as I knelt at that holy altar and,
clothed in the robes of the priesthood, took my husband's
hand and received a beautiful child of God to be our own.

Our son, dressed in his white suit, looked like an
angel as he was placed on the alter where his chubby little hand was grasped with our own in the eternal sealings
of a family. His brown eyes took in the whole scene as if
he completely understood each word being said.

Tears of joy ran down my face as I realized what a
great blessing was ours. Our son was "not a gift, but a
precious loan," a loan which carries a great responsibility,
but oh, so much joy.

The Blessing

Soon after President L. Tom Perry had been called to be an Assistant to the Twelve, I had occasion to visit with him in his office. I seemed to have a lot of problems to unload and he listened and he counseled and he gave me a blessing. As I was sitting listening to the blessing, I noticed that his hands were sliding down my head and he was very relaxed. I stopped listening and a feeling came over me that I knew to be complete joy. I don't remember what President Perry said from that moment because of the feeling I was having—a feeling of indescribable sweetness. I want to so live that I may be close enough to the Lord to have such a feeling of joy again.

The Power of Healing

An experience of faith and prayer that has brought me great joy since it happened came following the birth of my second daughter in a New York hospital. It was a breach birth and the pediatrician said the obstetrician had evidently pulled down on the baby's shoulder and caused a nerve injury. He told me her arm would turn outward and shrivel. Any mother can appreciate my feelings at that time. Her arm was put in a brace and each morning I was to give her exercises. I decided that I would do all my faith could accomplish, as my patriarchal blessing said that in conjunction with my companion, I could heal the sick in my household. Every morning after the baby's bath, my oldest little girl age four and I would pray to the Lord as I massaged and exercised the baby's arm with consecrated oil. After some months I will never forget the day when I excitedly said to my daughter, "Did you think she raised her arm a little?" Breathlessly we watched and suddenly the baby raised it again! Her arm did not wither and no one would know today she had any trouble. The nerves in the top of her arm and in a line down her arm do not have feeling, but she has capitalized on that by having any shots put there where she can't feel it. This has indeed been one of many strong testimonies on the power of healing within our family.

Here and Now

Our neighbors had a baby girl who was very ill and they sent for the doctor. He examined her and said it is just a matter of time and she will die. The parents felt bad and they called the bishop and myself to help administer to her. The doctor said, "She is dead now, so there is no need to do it." The bishop said, "No, she isn't." We administered to her and he promised her she would get well and be a mother in Zion. The doctor afterwards said she was dead, and a nurse in attendance said to the parents in order to comfort them, "Bishop S. means she will be well and be a mother in the next life." At that, the bishop said, "No, I mean here and now." The baby had been blue and to the natural eye she was dead. Now she is a mother and a beautiful woman.

A Miracle

My son had his own car, a 1971 Buick. I worried as most parents do for their children. I earnestly prayed for him that he would not hurt anyone with his car and that no one would hurt him. In April of 1974, he had five of his friends in the car. On a secondary oiled paved road down below Hurricane, he was taking some of his friends home. They came to a turn in the road. There was a 16-inch gravel shoulder between the oiled road and a canal. As he tried to make the turn, his front wheel hit the shoulder and it pulled him in the canal. The car went end over end, slid down the canal, and hit a big rock. When it stopped, the top was completely smashed flat. The kids all crawled out. One girl cut her arm crawling out of the back window which required four stitches. The rest didn't even have a bruise or scratch. Though none had their seat belts fastened, not one was thrown out of the car. We knew it was a miracle and everybody that looked at the car said, "That sure was a miracle those kids weren't killed."

The Lord has been so good to me. I feel most unworthy of all He has blessed me with. I love Him and give Him credit for answering my prayers.

My People

When I was twenty years old, I received my patriarchal blessing which states "your kindred dead have been waiting long for you to set them free from their prison house." I can still recall the feeling I had when the patriarch said those words. The feeling was "Please, Heavenly Father help me to succeed for them. Don't let me let my people down."

My people were all from Sweden and Denmark so I asked a lady who was doing research to help me out. As we looked from books to films, I had the feeling this wasn't right, so I went into a corner and asked my Heavenly Father to help me start my life's mission. I walked over and pulled a film drawer open and without a knowledge of Swedish, I found my grandmother's birthplace and her father and mother with six children.

One of the most rewarding experiences came after I had worked in genealogy for two years. I had looked for my grandfather's birthplace without success. One day after fasting all day, I felt my ancestor was real close to me. I went to work at BYU and found a major breakdown that made it so I had to go downtown for a part. On my way back I noticed a book laying in the road with its pages blowing in the wind. The feeling came over me to pick up the book. But I reasoned that it was dirty, it was torn, and nobody picks up books laying in the road. However, as I came near the book the feeling became so strong that I jumped out and picked up the latest copy of the Improvement Era. It had an article telling about genealogy records that were now available from Sweden.

Within an hour after I arrived in the archives, I had my grandfather's birthplace.

She Accepted

My husband's family are non-members and at the time we went back East to visit his grandmother, I was not in any way an active Mormon. But for an unknown reason, I felt compelled to do my husband's grandmother's side of the genealogy. I never before had an interest in or even knew much about genealogy. However, we spent that entire day and most of the night digging up information. My husband's grandmother called nearby relatives and even a daughter came to help. It was our only time with grandma. She cried when we left. Three months later she died unexpectedly.

When I came back to the church and, my husband joined, we felt compelled to do grandmas work. Right before we left for my husband's first assignment to Germany, we were married in the temple. I worked up a family sheet for his grandma so we could do the temple work for her, but I was unable to find the exact date of her death. We tried several sources but to no avail. We had almost given up. In trying to get a big book out of a shelf in my mother-in-law's home, I glanced at the Bible but decided to take the big dictionary instead to press some flowers that my MIA class gave me. But when I began pulling the book out, the Bible fell out. The Bible was at the other end, so it was no accident. It opened up to a page that had his grandmother's birth, DEATH, etc.,

listed! We did her work for her when we got to Europe, at
the Swiss Temple. I felt unusually elated during the
whole session and sealing. I knew she accepted it.

Family History, Answered Prayers

There was the time when I had spent days trying to
find where my husband's Adam's ancestry fitted in. On
one particular day I had worked all day in the Los Angeles
Library. At 4 p.m., I gathered up my papers and started to
leave. At the door, something directed me to a shelf in
the corner to my left. There were some old books there
that I had never noticed before. I picked up one and the
index showed an Archelaus. There was just one short sentence. "Archelaus Adams was a member of the snowshoe
militia in Newberry, Massachusetts." That location
opened up history that helped greatly in establishing this
ancestry. Our spirits soared and there was no doubt in our
minds but that this came as an answer to our prayers.

Another time we were driving along the road toward
Cincinnati when suddenly my husband turned onto a
side road for no reason we knew about. There was a small
sign there indicating one of the old burial mounds was on
the road. We found a small park nearby and a woman sitting on a bench while children played near her. In talking
to her, we found that she lived in Rocky River, Ohio, near
Cleveland, just across the street from distant cousins. We
learned from her that an aged cousin was still alive and in
fair health and that her mind was still clear. We immediately went to Cleveland and there we learned several

things that helped us. Again we knew that we were led there as an answer to our prayers.

The Power of the Priesthood

My mind goes back to the first experience I had with the power of the priesthood in my life, when I was in junior high school and had an accident that seriously burned my face with second-and third-degree burns.

The doctors were of the opinion that the burns would heal faster and more thoroughly if they were exposed to open air, but I presented a rather grotesque sight to myself and I was sure to others. I was just becoming aware of my own appearance and was very self-conscious as most young teens are.

My father and another priesthood bearer gave me a blessing that no noticeable scars would stay after the burns had healed. That very night as my mother treated the burns, which included a massage with a swab covered with petroleum jelly, the outer layers of skin that I was so ashamed of simply peeled off in large sections, revealing smooth, unblemished skin that was a delight for me to behold.

I am sure that it was the power of the priesthood and my own faith in that power that effected this miraculous recovery that my physicians were at a loss to explain.

A Spiritual Moment

I fell in a thorn bush and got thorns stuck in my legs. I couldn't walk because there was this one, big sticker. I prayed that Father in Heaven would cure me of this thing and make me walk. He did and I think this was a very spiritual moment for me.

"Will I Be Blind?"

In 1972, I left home with two of my sons, ages ten and sixteen, for a day of archery deer hunting in the mountains of Millard County. It was 8:15 as we reached the top of the ridge and one boy was looking at deer tracks in the soft dirt in the trail. I was holding my bow with a hunting arrow knocked in it at my side and in my left hand. Darwin was bent over looking at tracks. Neither of us realized that we were close to each other. I moved my bow just as he turned and looked up. I didn't feel the arrow touch anything and was not aware of what had happened when I saw him holding his eye with his hand. I asked if he had something in his eye. Not hearing his answer, my other son repeated that my arrow had hit him. I lay down my bow and arrow and kneeled at his side but couldn't see any blood on his closed eye or face. His eye was watering so I took my fingers and gently opened his eyelids. Till my dying day I will always see the cut in the center of his eye and the water running down his cheek. The cornea of his eye was punctured.

Then I said to myself, "Dear God, please help us!"

Then I thought, first we need the healing power of the priesthood. I asked Doug to place his hands on his brother's head with mine and we gave him a blessing, asking also for God's help and guidance. As I finished and lifted my hands, my panicked mind became clear and I knew what I had to do. At the same moment Darwin looked up and said, "Dad, will I be blind?" I felt impressed to promise him that he wouldn't be blinded, but that we had to get him to an eye specialist in a hurry. Nothing in the world could have brought me more comfort or reassurance at that minute than did the power of the priesthood, which my son and I felt so strongly. I told Doug to wait at the appointed place for the other two, tell them of the accident and that someone would pick them up later in the afternoon.

I put two large bandages over my son's eye, led him off the ridge to the truck and drove off the mountain as quickly as possible. I stopped at Scipio long enough to make a call to my brother in Holden and a call to my wife in Provo to line up an eye specialist and to meet me at the freeway exit to direct me to the doctor.

The eye was operated on by 2:00 p.m. but the doctor didn't give us too much hope. The arrow had gone in to the retina and the lens had to be removed. After one year and three operations and a lot more prayer and pleading, Darwin has 20-50 vision with the help of a special contact lens and a perfectly normal looking eye. The power of the priesthood has a very special meaning in our family. Only we as mortals limit its power by our lack of faith.

If Not Appointed Unto Death

As a boy I went to rake hay for my brothers Parley and Able. I was raking with a spirited team when the neck yoke broke dropping the tongue to the ground. The frightened team began to run and kick. The last I remember were the horses' hooves flying up in my face. One connected with my jaw and knocked me out. I fell forward and under the rake and stayed under the rake with hay and the dirt team running as fast as they could for nearly one-fourth of a mile. I guess the tongue of the rake broke and went in the ground enough to raise the rake to let me out. Then the rake and team hit a fence with four barbed wires and cedar posts and rolled wire. It broke seventeen cedar posts out. Had I been in the rake then I would have been cut and mashed to pieces. A lady saw the runaway and quickly phoned the doctor and then my folks. They could not tell front from back on me. Thinking I was dead they rolled me under the fence. I don't know who administered to me, but when I came to the doctor was finishing sewing my jaw. I know God means what he says; if not appointed unto death they shall recover by being anointed and administered to.

A Miracle

When I was three years of age, my mother, an older sister and I were living at the old Murdock Academy just east of Beaver, Utah. Mother was helping financially while my father was away at medical school. Two small children there at the academy came down with spinal meningitis and I was one. All the student body and faculty fasted two days and prayed for us. Mother used to tell me that my head was so hot at times that it almost burned her hand when she touched me. Brother Partridge was at this time teaching at the academy and Mother went to him and asked him to please pray for me and please come to the house to administer to me. He walked to a nearby grove and talked to the Lord, then he came to administer. I began at once to recover and recovered completely with no after effects at all. To me, from a doctor's family and myself a bacteriologist with a pre medic background, this truly is a miracle.

Choosing a Scout Master

Once, when I was serving as counselor to the bishop, we were faced with the problem of choosing a new Scoutmaster. That should not have been such a difficult task, but try as we would we could not come up with the right man. We deliberated and prayed about it, but each time we delayed action because we could not feel satisfied. Finally, as we sat one Sunday morning in our council meeting the action came. Neither of the bishopric yet had a name to propose but our ward clerk who always sat in on our meetings spoke up with this suggestion. "Brethren, release me from this position and I'll take the job."

Now this man was a good ward clerk but quite a joker. The other counselor and I laughed at his "joke." The bishop, however, was very sober and serious about the suggestion. After a few silent moments he said, "Brethren, I believe that is our answer." He spoke with a feeling of surety as one inspired.

The decision was made; this man made a fine Scoutmaster. We found another clerk, and were very grateful for guidance we had received.

Protected

During the year of 1971, I was employed by theaters in Hollywood, California. Because of the nature of Hollywood, there are people with various backgrounds and a variety of ages. This was my first job away from home and Hollywood held a certain fascination for me because I had led a somewhat sheltered life. One of the girls that worked with me had just moved from Virginia with her older sister who was twenty-five. They, like many, had come to California to find their fortunes. Like the rest of the employees, Patricia was involved with the use of drugs to some extent. I enjoyed her company and thought by fellowshipping her she would become interested in the church.

When we were together, drugs were never a part of our interaction because she knew I didn't believe in using them and she respected my decision. We used to have long talks about God and the purpose of life. One afternoon during July, I was visiting at her apartment. A few friends were over, also, but they were in the kitchen and we were in the living room. On the coffee table was sitting a water pipe just like the ones I'd seen in gift shops on Hollywood Blvd. The noise from the kitchen began to increase. For the first time I began to feel very uncomfortable sitting in the apartment talking with her. I began to feel like I should leave, but I kept telling myself this was nonsense and continued my conversation. The longer I remained the worse it got. As the noise increased, Gina yelled for Patrice to come into the kitchen. When she left the room, it was as if I had been struck with a bolt of lightning.

I don't really remember getting up from my chair. I was out the door and running frantically down Franklin Blvd. to Highland Ave. where my car was parked. People on the street were giving me looks of concern.

Upon reaching my car I felt a warmth come over me from head to foot. It had been overcast and cold which was unusual for a July day. I knew the feeling that I was experiencing was that of the Holy Ghost. In my heart, I knew something was wrong, but I also knew I wasn't to return to find out. I felt as if my life had been in danger and in a sense it had.

For the next two days Patricia didn't show up at work. I dropped by the apartment but no one was home. Finally after a few days went by Patricia stopped by the theater. She had been in jail along with the rest of the people in her apartment. Just a few minutes after I had left, the apartment was raided by the Los Angeles Police Department Narcotics Division. One of her sister's friends was a pusher and they had been watching him for a long time. Everyone in the kitchen was loaded on smack.

This experience was a great testimony builder for me.

I felt very blessed that the Lord had enough love and concern for me to help me stay out of trouble I wasn't looking for. Now that I'm older, I really am grateful for the many blessings the gospel has brought into my life. As I look back, if I had been in the apartment, my life would have been ruined. Telling an officer that you were only an innocent bystander would have made him laugh.

I know that by living the principles of the gospel that my parents, grandparents and Church leaders have taught me I truly can experience joy, because I will be in tune with the Lord and he will guide and protect me.

The Spirit

It was on a Tuesday while I was serving as bishop of the Santa Rosa Ward that I was asked to conduct a funeral on Friday for someone who had no church affiliation. By Wednesday, all assignments had been made–speaker, prayers, pallbearers, organist, and special music, two vocal solos.

During Thursday night my sleep was disturbed to the point that I did not rest well, and I had the definite feeling that something was not in order. My thoughts surveyed everything that might be involved and by a process of elimination I decided it must be something associated with the funeral. So as soon as I awakened I started calling to confirm all the assignments for the funeral that day. Each one involved said that he was prepared and would be there until I called the soloist. His response was "I am so glad you called, I knew I had something special to do today but it was not on my calendar." He had not been at home where he kept his appointment book when he accepted this assignment.

The Prompting

I had an experience when the prompting of the Spirit saved my little boy's life. He was taking a nap in his crib, as usual in the afternoons when he was about two years old. By this time he had torn the binding off his blanket enough to wrap it around his neck and twist it. He was unable to undo it or to yell for help. Contrary to my usual habit, for I normally wouldn't check on him until he got settled down longer, I felt a strong urge to go to him. When I reached him he had passed out and his face was near purple. I undid the wrapping just in time to restore his breathing.

He Said They Should Wait

My father was a member of the general board of the MIA for nearly twenty years. In those days, the members of the different boards of the Church would travel to the different stakes in the Church to attend their stake conferences. One time my father was in Arizona on an assignment. Their meetings were completed earlier than expected. My father asked the visiting general authority if they could catch an earlier flight back to Salt Lake City. He said they should wait for their originally scheduled flight which they did.

Upon landing in Salt Lake City they received word that the plane which left earlier had gone down over Nevada. My father said that experiences such as this taught him to never question the words or suggestions of the general authorities.

Loved Enough to Believe

When I was a junior in high school around seventeen years old, I felt strong spiritual and social needs. I had grown up in a good LDS home and had a basic belief in God, but my yearnings exceeded the walls of my home.

I felt a need to test the gospel to see if it was true enough that I could base my security on it for the rest of my life. I looked for hypocrisy in my church peers and the church adults. I felt that if the church was true, then the members would really love each other and love me. I also wanted to find out if there was a spiritual power or testimony.

I, in my prosecuting sort of way, tested the belief of my church friends and thought up everything negative I could against the church. I was very fortunate to have friends with strong testimonies and patient natures. Each time I would criticize the gospel, they would lovingly bear their testimonies concerning the subject. I would refute their answers for the moment because of pride, but weeks later I found myself preaching the same truths they bore to me.

I became sensitive to the spirituality of my friends and sought for the same inner glow. Their love and concern had touched me. Because they loved me, I believed that there is a God that loves me and is concerned about my affairs. Feeling loved by my friends, I sought to love God and receive of his great charity. I found that this love of God and others is the greatest joy of my whole life. I desired to feel more of this charity and thus prayed long hours and read the Book of Mormon and other scriptures diligently.

But most of all, my heart' turned to serve others and to pray for them, that somehow they would feel loved enough to believe in a God that loves them and in a gospel of love that I enjoy.

A Closeness That Was Unexpected

My greatest joys in belonging to the Church have been from the closeness of friendships with people in and out of the Church, aided through the Spirit in some cases. The Holy Ghost helps you to get closer to people, to be more loving, and opens doors for missionary work and for helping others.

In early January, 1974, I was hitchhiking around the West Coast and was picked up by a guy (and a bunch of other people) in a Volkswagen van. He was driving and I was in the back so I didn't get to talk with him until we got to San Diego (about 30 miles). There, he let someone else drive so he could "rap with the hitchhikers." El Cajon, where I was going, is only about 15 miles from San

Diego, but he started talking to me. I told him I was from Utah, and he commented that he was once in Salt Lake in a restaurant and he thought the waitress was a Mormon. I said that I was a Mormon, and he asked me to tell him about the Church because he didn't know anything at all about it. I told him about Joseph Smith and the Book of Mormon and gave my testimony. I found out he was a Christian Jew and he said he would like to read the Book of Mormon. I asked him if he would like for me to send him one and he said yes. Now we were in El Cajon and I had to leave. We got out and shook hands, then put our arms around each other and I told him that I sure loved him and he would be hearing from me, and then we said good-bye.

It was such a good feeling between us. Here I had talked to him for maybe fifteen minutes, and yet we both felt the Spirit and a closeness, that was unexplainable. I was just so happy to be telling him about the Church, too. (I have sent him a Book of Mormon and a letter, and am referring him to the missionaries in Florida, where he is now. I think there's a real good chance he'll join the Church.)

Setting an Example

Soon after I returned home from school I received a letter in the mail from the coordinator for LDS girls camp asking me to be music director for the one week camp. This calling really excited me, so I began to plan immediately. By the time camp came, I had many exciting things planned, and hoped to display to "my girls" (as I soon called them) my enthusiasm to sing with them.

During the week, one particular incident really had a tremendous effect on me. One day I saw one of the girls sitting way off in a field, so I went to see if anything was wrong. She told me that she could not describe the feeling she had right then, but the tears were streaming down her face. Finally she admitted that one of the young men who had come to assist me during one of my programs had hurt her feelings, but then she said, "I don't know if he really hurt me." Well, I thought I would make her feel better by telling her what a bum he really was and not to pay any attention to him. That's when the surprise came to me. She lifted her head, and stopped crying. She said that she couldn't believe I had really said that. She said she had never heard me say anything bad about anyone, and wondered if I had really meant it.

It then dawned on me that through the days at camp I had set an example to this thirteen year-old sister, and no doubt the other sisters. The faith this sister had in me was suddenly shot down by one little sentence. So I suggested to her that we pray, and I apologized to her, to the young man, and to my Father in Heaven for false judgement. That was the most beautiful and special feeling I have ever received from a prayer.

The Mission

Although there are eight children in our family, I somehow was closest to one brother. We played together when we were little, and then when I went to college, it was he who, when I got to go home, would take me out shooting, or to the park, the beach or the Queen Mary. That's why when he and another brother started drifting away from the church, my heart just about broke. For two years I worried, along with my parents; but all we could do was to do our best as examples and pray that the boys would come through in the end. During these two years I seemed to gain more and more of my testimony, and wrote often of little incidents in my life when I sent letters home. One year around Thanksgiving time I suddenly became obsessed with a desire to go home—it was all I could think about—I was more homesick as a graduate student than I had ever been as a freshman. Then, late one night, he called. He wanted me home for Thanksgiving, he said, and what's more, he had saved his money so I could fly home. It was that Thanksgiving that Jim took me for a long ride, and told me not to say anything to anyone; but he thought he would be going on a mission, and he was saving his money for that purpose.

I wish you could imagine the real joy I felt the day Mom called and told me that the night before my brother had called a special Family Home Evening to tell the family that he really was going to go on a mission, and that it was because of me that he had made this decision. I don't know when I have ever felt more humbled.

Now, beginning his mission at age twenty-one, he writes: "I want to bear my testimony to you that this—

The Church of Jesus Christ—is the true and the only church of Christ...The Lord has so much to offer us and he asks so little."

An "Impossible" Line

The Lord has shown his power through genealogical research. For example, my mother told me I could never do anything on my great-grandfather's line because he was bound out at the age of five, and never knew his parents. When in the Midwest in the summer of 1967, I did everything I could to find the origin of this man. Finally, at the Iowa State Department of History and Archives, I was prompted to look for an obituary on him in the newspaper collection there. They had no paper of the little town where he lived, but they did have a complete file of the Albia Union-Republican, the county seat paper. I searched those pages for a month after his death date, but found nothing, and was about to give up when I saw at last what I had been looking for: "John B. Hufford was born in Washington County, Pennsylvania." Since I had already planned to go to eastern Ohio on that trip, I extended the route to take me to western Pennsylvania, and there, again by use of a last resort in the local deed books, found the whole family and have since pushed that "impossible" line back into the sixteenth century. I had prayed, hoped, and worked a great deal to find this precious information, and the Lord answered my prayers in his own time and in his own miraculous way.

The Baptism

This happened to me while I was in the mission field in Canada. Sometime, about within the first month that I was out, my companion and I had made arrangements to baptize a lady. Her husband put up quite a resistance to her being baptized. He physically abused her and made things generally difficult for her. But she decided that she would be baptized because she knew the truthfulness of the gospel and she was bound and determined to be baptized under any circumstances. The only place we had to baptize her was in the YMCA swimming pool. This was in November, and the swimming pool had not been used for approximately three months. Consequently, the water was very cold. In fact, the only reason there was water in the pool was so the ground frost wouldn't crack the concrete in the pool. This November in particular it was about 30 degrees below zero. The water in the pool couldn't have been much above freezing.

On the day of the baptism this lady came to me about five minutes before we were to baptize her and related the following incident. She said, "I just got back from my doctor's and he advised me not to be baptized." She proceeded to tell me that she had a very weak heart, and the doctor felt that if the water was cold at all when she was baptized that she would die of a heart attack.

When she told me this, I as a young, green missionary, nearly panicked. I went to my companion and said, "What are we going to do? We can't baptize her or she'll die."

He answered, "Don't worry, Elder. The Lord takes care of his own." That was easy for him to say because I was the one that was supposed to baptize her, and I would be the one to hold her as she died.

The time for the baptism came. I stepped down in the water, and it was so cold that it took my breath away. The deeper I went into the water, the colder it got. I could picture the lady lying on the bottom of the pool dead.

After I was all the way in the water, I turned around to put my hand out for her to come into the water for her baptism. The second she put her foot into the water, that water turned warm. It was so warm that she didn't gasp once. She didn't act startled in any way. You could not tell that the water had been cold at all.

I baptized her—everything went fine. After she had come up out of the water, she proceeded to the stairway. The second her foot left the water, that water was once again so cold that it made me gasp for breath just as if someone had thrown a glass of ice water on me. I couldn't get out of the swimming pool fast enough.

After the baptism was over, I asked her, "Was the water too cold for you?"

She replied, "No. It was just right, It was just about the same as I take my bath in."

I know how cold that water was. My companion knew how cold that water was, and the Lord knew how cold it was. But her faith was strong enough that it didn't matter.

A Barefooted Child

While tracting in a wooded area of California in 1941, my companion and I encountered a woman living in a

dirty trailer home, very small but with many small, barefooted children running around the wooded swamp area
outside. The mother, a Finnish woman, accepted us and
we taught her the gospel. Her husband was working away
and we never met him. The sister was baptized. I was
transferred and I never heard any more of the family until
in 1949.

I had just graduated from BYU and was moving with
my wife and new baby into a rented home off campus
when the doorbell rang. A strange and beautiful young
woman said to my wife," Is your husband here?" My wife
said, "Yes, he is putting up a bed in the back bedroom. "
The young lady pushed past my wife and marched on
through to me in the back bedroom. In a moment of
unspeakable joy I discovered that she was the daughter of
the sister in California. In 1941, she was a barefooted
child running loose around the trailer house. She had just
come to Salt Lake City from Northern California to be
married in the temple and wanted so much to share this
with the missionary who brought the gospel to her
mother.

The Miracle Village in Taiwan

On the morning of April 1, 1973, I left with my companion and the mission president for an obscure little
fishing village in Southern Taiwan. Our assignment was
to open the new village for proselyting and then to baptize some 200 souls who were followers of a minister of a

little protestant chapel in the village.

The minister's fifteen-year-old daughter, Julie, was a recent convert to the Mormon Church. She had met the elders while working away from home in an industrial city. There, the Book of Mormon brought a testimony of truth to her of the restored gospel of Jesus Christ and she desired to be baptized.

Her father opposed her baptism quite sternly, but through the prayers of her tremendous faith and through much fasting, she touched her father's heart with the deep, soul-inspiring words of the Book of Mormon. He began teaching his own congregation the new beautiful truths he had learned. He preached of authority yet to come to them and of a restoration that had come to the earth through a prophet.

At the request of the minister, we came to teach and lead his congregation into the waters of baptism. Little Julie glowed with joy as she watched the gospel touch the lives of the people she loved so much. She witnessed sixty of her villagers baptized that day! The following week, fifty-two more joined the fold. Through the fervent testimony of one fifteen-year-old Chinese girl an entire branch was organized among the simple farmers and fishermen of the miracle village in Taiwan.

The Northwestern States Mission

While serving my mission in the Northwestern States mission, I was transferred to Oregon. While there, my companion and I taught a family that was brought into the Church–all except the husband. An older lady of our ward lived across the street. Because of the friendship she had with the missionaries and her neighbor there was concern when she wasn't seen for a couple of days.

The sister called us and asked if we would see if she was okay or on a trip. When we went by her house, there were three days' papers and milk. We knocked, but no answer. After a few moments we tried the door. We found it locked but not pushed shut hard enough. Coincidence? We opened the door slightly and called out for her. We heard a rattle in the bedroom and some mumbling so we thought she was getting ready to come out to see us. After a small wait we again called to her and mentioned we were the missionaries. We repeated this three times in all and finally went into the room to find her lying on the floor. We found out she had a stroke three days prior and whenever she heard us call she would try to move, only to kick the sliding doors of her closet. We came into the room and finding her there we lifted her up on the bed and gave her a blessing. We called her doctor and got a neighbor to help take her to the hospital. By the time we got her there she was talking to us. My faith in the power of healing was greatly increased that day and will stay with me forever.

"I Have Waited So Long For You"

As I think about the phrase "Men are that they might have joy," I am reminded of the great joy of service which I experienced as a missionary to the Lamanite people in

Arizona and New Mexico. Never have I known such joy in serving others. Up to that point, I had only known the shallow joy of self-servitude.

In the latter part of my mission I had one of my choicest experiences. As part of our tracting one day, my companion and I contacted a family in the low-rent housing district. The members of this family greeted us warmly and asked us to come in. As we introduced ourselves and the message we had brought that day, the mother began to cry. Both my companion and I were so touched that we stopped the discussion and after a few moments of silence I asked her what was wrong. She replied with only one sentence, "I have waited so long for you." We ended our discussion without hardly any more said and set up another appointment.

As we went through the lessons with the good family her words kept being repeated in my brain and as she and her husband and children were baptized, I thought of those words again. I thought of the joy I would have missed if I had failed in my service to the Lord the joy for which this family would have had to wait longer.

The Thing That Saved Us

My companion and I were scheduled for a district meeting about sixty miles away from our area. As we prepared for our journey the night before, we loaded what supplies we would need. Since we were in charge of distributing the Book of Mormons to the other elders in the zone, we loaded what books we knew they needed. As we awoke earlier the next morning, we discovered about six inches of new snow. We decided to try and make the meeting anyway. After we had prayer and were preparing to leave for the car, a small voice whispered to us to take all the cases of the Book of Mormon we had and put them in the car. We didn't know why, but we did as we were prompted to do. The road was icy and very slick.

About half way to our destination our car went out of control and we hit the guard rail. A man in a semi stopped and said he'd get help about one mile further up the road. Since it was so cold, we were sitting in the car while help came. We both still had our seat belts fastened as we waited. The same voice prompted us to remove our seat belts and to slump down in the seat. We did this without hesitation. We no sooner done what we were told than a car crashed into the back of us going 70 miles per hour. The impact threw our car up and almost over the guard rail. The front seat busted and we were forced into the back of the car. It totaled the car, but we were unhurt except for a few bruises and a cracked nose that my companion received. The thing that saved us were the cases of the Book of Mormon in the trunk of the car. Many books were ripped through the center. Some were ripped to pieces. The patrol officer said he couldn't understand how we were so lucky not to be hurt. It was a testimony to us to listen to the promptings of the still small voice.

My Friend

When I was twenty-three I was employed as a restaurant manager for a chain store back east. I had just graduated from their restaurant's training program and was transferred to my first "unit" in New Jersey. The first week was really hectic. On a Friday we received our pay, and, believe me, that first week I felt I had really earned every penny of mine. We received our pay in cash. Mine was $125.00. I had my dinner in the restaurant that evening with the manager and two assistant managers of the store. I had taken my pay envelope and laid it on the table next to my plate, having taken it out of my pocket.

One of the cooks was on his dinner break and the other cook started getting busy. Instinctively I jumped up to help him. I was only gone for about ten minutes, but when I returned my pay was gone. It was a foolish thing for me to do, and there was nothing to do about it. I couldn't accuse the people at the table; they were store management, but one of them had taken it. I really felt sick, no money (I needed that money to get an apartment) and no friends, in this new town.

The next day one of the assistant managers who was off the day of the incident approached me. He said he heard my pay was stolen and asked if I needed to borrow any money from him or if there was anything he could do for me.

He was a complete stranger, and I was to him, yet he trusted me enough to offer to loan me money. Fortunately my parents sent me money but the Lord sent me a friend and at the time that was more important.

That person was the greatest human being I ever met

(and still is). He's kind and considerate, sincerely concerned about people, humble, and humorous, a really gen-
tle man. He was a "peculiar person." He didn't drink,
smoke, drink coffee or tea, or swear, which was really
unusual for people in that area. We were friends for a
whole year before we ever talked about religion. He said,
"What church do you belong to?" I said, "Episcopal." He
said, "Do you believe in God?" I said, "Yes." "How about
Christ?" I said, "No." He said, "Well, what do you think
happens when you die?" I said, "Nothing." He said,
"Nothing' That's awful: What are you living for?" I said,
"I don't know, I never thought of it that way." He said,
"I'll give you something to live for, I'll send some friends
of mine over to tell you about my church."

Little did I know it was Mormon missionaries he was
sending, or that three months later my friend would baptize me into the church, or that he would influence me to
apply for college and one year later I'd be studying art.

My friend surely gave me something to live for, and he
and his family have changed the course of my whole life
through their good examples.

The Film

During my mission in Northern Denmark a number
of years ago, I had taken some colored slides of the birthplace of my grandfather. My companion and I had travelled to an out-of-the-way place just to take these pictures. I was extremely well pleased that I had this opportunity. After returning to the place where we lived, I

mailed the film to Copenhagen for processing. Weeks passed and the developed film never arrived. I sent several letters to inform them, but the film company claimed they mailed them days ago. Since these pictures were of value to me and my family, the only recourse was to turn to the Lord. I prayed and fasted and then left things in the hands of the Lord.

One evening a member of our branch was visiting some friends in another part of the Pity. These friends showed him some colored slides and she recognized my companion and me. The next Sunday at sacrament meeting she told us about seeing the pictures. These films turned out to be my own, and I soon had them back in my possession. Except for a few finger marks, they were in good condition. What had happened was the film had been delivered to the wrong address—the home of a shoemaker. He had given the film to a young boy—a customer. He had taken them home, thinking they were a toy. Just by coincidence they had been shown to the branch member.

Our Prayer Was Heard

An experience I remember that brought me great joy and also an increased awareness of my position happened to me while serving a mission in Denmark. We had made the acquaintance of an older gentleman. Agreeing to meet the man and the circumstances under which we met were of themselves very unusual. We had visited him several times and had given him two or three of the missionary lessons. He was proceeding quite well and seemed to be eating up everything we gave him. I remember the first time we asked him to pray. He gave a very beautiful and simple prayer.

One day as we returned for our scheduled appointment, he complained of an acute pain in the back and asked if we might meet on another day. As we talked for a few moments, I felt inspired to ask him if we could give him a blessing. This was the first time I had ever done this to a nonmember. Normally I wouldn't have even thought of it except for the fact that this man had such a great faith in God and he believed what we had taught him. I briefly explained to him what a blessing was and he said, yes, he would very much appreciate such a blessing.

As we laid our hands on his head, I felt a power surge through my chest which I had never experienced before. The words flowed freely from my lips and I knew our prayer was being heard. As we ended, he had tears in his eyes and we were both kind of speechless. We were out on the street and mounted our bikes in silence.

We didn't see him for a few days and it got so I was almost afraid to see him again because of my lack of faith in our prayers. Finally we met him, and the first thing he told us was of how about ten minutes after we had left after giving him the blessing, his pain had left and had not returned. To say the least this experience strengthened my testimony in the power of the priesthood and prayer.

The Rain Stopped

Of all the experiences that have brought me joy, perhaps the one that is most memorable to me is an incident that happened while on my mission in England. During part of my mission I was a member of a missionary singing group called the "Family Album." We traveled throughout the mission putting on shows for large gatherings of members and investigators. Needless to say we had many choice experiences, but the one I relate is, to me, a very special experience.

We were in an area of London known as Greenwich for the purpose of performing an outdoor concert, but, as often is the case in England, the weather was not cooperating. We arrived at the concert site and sat silently in the van for a moment listening to the rain pound on the roof. Obviously the concert could not be held outside so we looked around the high-rise apartments for the tenant's association hall. We found a hall that we could have used but it was much too small. We returned to the van. The chorus of raindrops on the roof seemed almost to mock us. We didn't want to cancel the concert, but it appeared as though we would have to. We were at a loss as to the course we should take.

As we had always been taught to pray when in need of guidance, we decided that would be the best thing to do at the time. We joined in prayer; Elder V. being voice, and asked for guidance. It came to us that we, as priesthood holders, have powers that enable us to accomplish the things that we have been called to do, even though they may seem impossible. We prayed again, the rain still creating a constant din on the roof of the van. This time, in

our prayer, we commanded by the power of the priesthood that the rain would cease. No sooner had we all said
"amen" than the rain stopped as suddenly as if someone
had turned off a faucet. Tears came to our eyes and gratitude to our hearts for the power of the priesthood.

We held our concert that evening—outdoors. I never
found out if anyone we contacted that night through our
performance was ever baptized, but to this day I am
thankful to the Lord for that experience that showed me,
beyond a doubt, the power of the priesthood.

Feeding the Missionaries

Rain, snow, sleet, or hail, the missionaries never failed
to come to dinner at our home in Lawrence, Kansas. We
had them over every Monday for dinner and games. We
kids could always win in any sport because we were the
ones to make the rules. We learned a lot from the missionaries and shared many experiences which enriched
our lives.

We did not have a lot of money at that time because
my father was going to school to get his Ph. D. One
Monday, Mother was complaining about not having
enough to eat that day. In the mail was a $10.00 bill with-
out a name or address on the paper it was enclosed in.
The place it was mailed from was Florida and we didn't
know anybody there at the time.

Mother bought the dinner and we had a good meal
that night. Nobody in our family has ever complained
about feeding the missionaries ever again.

It All Came Back

While in the army I was stationed in Ft. Myer, Virginia. On my way to Church I had to walk through the Arlington National Cemetery in order to get to the bus stop where I could catch a ride to Church. On my way, I encountered several people in a Volkswagen who sought my assistance in finding a telephone. As the nearest phone was right by the bus stop, I caught a ride with them to that site. The couple in the front of the vehicle informed me that the older gentleman in the back seat had just lost a son in the Vietnam War and had been so shaken that he lost his memory, and couldn't even find the location of his house. He seemed to be dazed. At the phone booth they called the house, but no one was home. I decided to guide them there, then walk to the nearest bus line, since I strongly sympathized with the father, knowing at that time that I, too, might end up as one of the victims of that conflict. Consequently, I guided them to the location. Then, as I was about to take my leave of them I felt very strongly a desire to bless the life of this man and help him if I could. I thought that they might not accept my offer of assistance if I mentioned who I was, so I merely said, "I was a missionary. Is there anything I can do?" To my surprise they asked if I would pray for them. So, I, along with the others, bowed my head in the street, which was quiet at that time of the Sunday morning, and I offered a prayer. When I finished the prayer, they thanked me, and I turned to go. But, as I moved to depart, the older man caught me by the arm and restrained me. With a clear look of full comprehension in his eyes he looked me straight in the eye and said,

"Thank you. It all came back. I remember everything!"

In Hawaii

I was living in Hawaii with my brother when I met
Mike, a sailor from Iowa. Mike was from a strong
Catholic family, but he told me how he didn't feel right
about Church and just never went when he was away
from home. But Mike was a good man. As a child he was
taught Catholic prayers and he believed in God. He was
active in scouting, having received his Eagle Scout. I
invited him to Church one Sunday morning, and I began
to share my testimony and the gospel with him. He had
many questions and a desire to know more, so I called in
the elders and the first week in July he began to have the
discussions.

He was interested and wanted to be baptized so he
called his folks and asked them about it. They tried to
discourage him. They told him to wait and find out about
plural marriage and our view on the negro and the priesthood. Mike decided to wait on his baptism. August 19, he
was leaving for California and I didn't know if I would see
him. For hours we talked; then we prayed together and
fasted, hoping he could get an answer. Three days later
the missionaries came to talk to him and Mike said, "Can
I be baptized August 18?" True joy was felt by all of us,
watching a wonderful man accept the gospel of Jesus
Christ.

The Healing

When a missionary in the Southern States mission, I had the opportunity of participating in the healing of a young nonmember. This seventeen year-old boy had a tragic mishap just before Christmas, 1968. While tying and curling a bow on a Christmas gift, he ran a pair of scissors completely through his eye. The doctor that treated him in the hospital told him that he would never see again in that eye. At this time he was dating a young LDS girl who had a strong testimony of the healing power of the priesthood. She called my companion and myself and asked us to give him a blessing.

As we laid our hands upon him, I was prompted to tell this young man that his sight would be restored. This was a very humbling experience for us. As we walked from the hospital we commented to each other that we had felt the Spirit and that our strength had been transferred into the boy's body. We commented on how weak we felt physically. I actually felt energy come from inside my body, go through my hands, and into his body. This power felt like an electric current and sent chills from my head to my feet. When the bandage was removed from the young man's eye, he had complete and total vision.

At the Language Training Mission

I have worked as a teacher at the Language Training Mission for three years. Some of the most courageous, faithful, humble people in the world are the young missionaries that come through the LTM (Language Training Mission existed prior to the Missionary Training Center) to learn a new language. About two years ago an Elder came into the mission that taught me a great lesson about faith. He was a great big boy. His dark hair was cut so that it hung over the frame of his glasses, which necessitated a constant shaking of the head. He had that glassy, far-away look in his eye that tells you he was really mixed up.

I took a special interest in him and by chatting with him before and after class, we became close buddies. His progress with the language was very slow and his memory was so poor that the possibility of memorizing the six discussions in Spanish seemed hopeless. One day I noticed that he was especially depressed and during the course of our chat he confessed to me that he knew that his problem stemmed from excessive drug abuse in his high school years. His was not just an occasional experience with marijuana, but a much more involved history of LSD and amphetamine usage. He had been told that his mind would never be any good and that the acid had blown his program. While he was at the peak of this drug experience he became acquainted with the Church and through proper therapy overcame his drug problem.

Now he was on a mission and faced with the challenge of learning a new language and memorizing over 200 pages of discussion material, and it seemed like an impossible task. We worked together and though he often got depressed, he never gave up. He used to say, "The Lord has called me, he will provide a way." After six weeks, his Spanish was still unintelligible and he was unable to repeat even one of the 200 pages of memorization. I was ready to give up, but he was still sure that he could do it. His final two weeks came and we decided to fast and pray for strength and for the ability to learn the discussions.

The next two weeks are still unexplainable. He suddenly got his memorizing power back and learned all of the required material. His ability with the language greatly improved and he left the LTM even more prepared than many of the young people that had normal learning capacities. I was a little ashamed of my lack of faith and dependence on the Lord. The letters I have received from this great missionary in the field assure me that the Lord has a great work in mind for him, a work that required this test of his faith and trust. What a truly great example this Elder has been for me.

The Blind Man

The Holy Ghost has been a great influence on my life. One time in the mission field, I had the opportunity to teach a blind man. For me this was quite an experience because it took me a year and a half to prepare myself through the help of the power of the Holy Ghost. As I first went to Japan, I had a distinct impression that I wanted to teach a blind person as I saw one walking down the street, but I rationalized my way out. I knew little Japanese; how could I explain anything if he couldn't see it? I was only a junior companion. I even mentioned it to my senior companion and he said the same things I had thought. I did this twice more in different areas and once as a senior companion, but always came to the same conclusions. Then in the last six months of my mission, I was transferred to my last branch. One day I saw a blind man as I was street contacting, but I turned and talked to someone else as he passed by. He turned around, and I bumped into him. There I was, but the thoughts of inadequacy rushed through my mind. I talked to him and he said he would come to Church. I was scared, but as the few weeks went on he learned the gospel and understood it better than most investigators. He now is helping others to understand the gospel.

Summer Reading

During the summer, I worked as a security guard in a seventeen story office building. The job involved a great deal of sitting so I decided to read Church books in all my spare time–something I had never taken the time to do before. The desk at which I sat was situated in the middle of the lobby and so tenants and visitors passed by and some would stop to chat or ask what I was reading. One particular stockbroker became interested when I told him I was reading a book called *Jesus the Christ*. I told him I attended BYU and he deducted that I was a "Mormon." After talking briefly about the Church, he committed me to bring him a Book of Mormon the next day. He began reading and doing some research on the side. The next day he called the bishop in his area for the time of Sunday meetings.

He enjoyed the services so much that a week later he decided to find out what it was that made this Church tick, so he planned a week-end trip to Salt Lake City. It turned out, one of the stake missionaries that was teaching him was going down that same weekend to send a niece off on a mission and offered to show him around. I told him to be sure to not miss the choir broadcast on Sunday morning and some other points of interest in Salt Lake.

Upon his return, I learned that not only did he attend the regular broadcast, but also a special program in memory of the late President Lee. The entire First Presidency was in attendance. Afterwards, he shook hands with all three men and carried on a short conversation with President Tanner who told him, "not to investigate the Church for too long." My friend took this advice. He finished the next six lessons in the following two weeks and was baptized a week later. My joy came at the water's edge as I witnessed this fine man accept the gospel and become baptized.

My Mother Realized

One of the greatest joys of my life was seeing my mother realize that the gospel was true and be baptized a member of the Church. My father was a "Jack Mormon" and I had attended Primary and Sunday School nearly all my life. My mother was Catholic (inactive) and always supported me in the Church, but never really took much of a personal interest.

One day a couple of brand new elders came to our home to visit. They didn't know Mom wasn't a member, and when they found out, they perked up. They became very close friends with our family and visited us often for several weeks. Then my father invited them over to dinner and said, "After dinner you can give us the first missionary discussion." What a surprise!

Mother took all the lessons and was baptized a few weeks later. All the years of trying to teach her and be an example to her had finally concluded in the great joy of seeing her baptized. It just took the right time in her life and the right pair of missionaries.

Since that time many sad things have happened to her in her life and she is still struggling with her testimony, but she has a good foundation and a great desire to become a strong member.

A Branch in Wisconsin

When I consider the ideals of joy in the lives of LDS people, I reflect upon the branch that I worked in while on my mission. The branch was located in Wisconsin. The active spirit in the branch was encouraging and uplifting to every member. I suppose the principal reason for the spirit of the branch lay in the attitude of the branch president who was actively coordinating the operation in such a way as to teach the members celestial principles. He backed his teachings by leading the kind of life which could be considered a model. In short, he was living and teaching the gospel as the prophets of the

Church have intended it to be carried out.

One other family particularly impressed me in that branch. They were a young couple with five children. They were much the same as any other family. They had squabbles between the children. They were not wealthy, but the parents had decided early in their marriage they would raise their family in accordance with gospel principles. So by the time we became acquainted with them, they had several year's experience. My heart was filled with joy to see their success. To begin with, they had taken Family Home Evening and implemented it to its full extent. Each family member was actively working on spiritual goals which had been decided in their home evenings. Responsibility for the home evenings were rotated so that each member of the family had his/her turn conducting, giving lessons, leading music, and giving prayers. The most exciting thing was the results. They knew and accepted the idea of leadership. They understood the goals that they were working on and were visibly making progress with them. The father of this family discovered another inroad lying within a principle that the Church has used for some time–the idea of personal interviews.

Each month he would call his sons into his bedroom and have a long personal talk with them individually. Even the youngest son was included. The amazing part was that he found that the boys took it very seriously. It became amazingly simple to approach such problems as sex education, school mate differences, personal failings and discouragement, continued strengthening of goals, and testimony. The parents often bore testimony to their children as the children also bore their testimonies to each other. My heart thrilled as I listened to one of the boys, approximately nine to ten years old bear his testimony in fast meeting and explain how much these goals and family home evenings were helping him to build his testimony. And I suppose the greatest thing about this family lies behind the purpose of my telling you about them—they had a true joy and peace about their home that could not be denied. One had but to enter their home to know that therein abided the spirit of the Lord and their joy. It is my firm conviction that true joy comes only from obedience to the principles life and salvation that God has revealed to us through his prophets.

A Father in Brazil

Perhaps the second greatest source of joy to me has been missionary experiences. That's a pretty broad category, but it's hard to pick out one or two. I especially remember one family who we worked with. The father had never learner to read (they lived in a rural area in Brazil) and was having a hard time getting a testimony since he couldn't read the Book of Mormon and there wasn't time at home for his family to read it to him. A member girl heard of the problem and began spending hours reading the Book of Mormon and missionary tracts into a tape recorder. Each night we would give the recorder to the man and he would listen to it during his job as a night watchman. His progress from then on was remarkable and a beautiful family entered the Church.

In Italy

I think that the greatest spiritual experience of my life came when I was a missionary in Italy. My companion and I worked very hard with a special family. They were to be the first members in a small town. The time came for them to live the Word of Wisdom, which for Italians is the ultimate sacrifice. We fasted and prayed very hard for this moment because we knew they had accepted it the night before, but they were being tempted by Satan to the utmost the next day.

We went and found that they hadn't been able to live the Word of Wisdom because the temptations were so strong. When I spoke to them, I suddenly was able to speak the most perfect Italian I had ever spoken and I used words and spoke more forcefully than I had ever spoken in my life. I was assured inside that the spirit had touched them and bore witness that the word of wisdom was true. We then had the most beautiful prayer together and we all received a burning assurance that they would make it and soon be baptized. Later trials came, but they always remembered that experience and that the Lord would always help when a sincere prayer was offered.

A Ring With a Red Stone

Prayer has been a great factor in my life. When I was a kid, my mother and dad gave me a beautiful ring for my birthday with a red stone that to me was a ruby. When I was playing on my grandmother's lawn, I somehow lost it. I started home crying and then decided to go back and pray for help to find it. By a lilac bush, I asked the Lord to help me find it. I went back to where I had been playing and soon found the ring.

Letter From My Son

A few years ago I had a serious illness and was facing surgery for cancer with the prospect that I might not be healed. I had many blessings given me, but the thing that gave me the most assurance was this letter I received from my son on the day I entered the hospital for the third operation:

Dearest Mom,
My thoughts have been continually with you and I know you are going to be A-OK.

It is hard and upsetting to one to know that someone you have loved so dearly all of your life is sick with an illness such as cancer and know that there is nothing physical you can do to help. After becoming aware of your illness and pondering it in my mind, I decided that I would leave the physical help up to your doctors, and I along with your other loved ones would seek the help of our Father in Heaven to do what only we can do.

Each day I have spent, as I know have Dad and your other children and grandchildren, much time on my knees talking with the Lord about your problem. He is aware of it and I know that He will help you. You are going to get along all right and have full recovery.

From day one, you and Dad have taught me that there is a Father in Heaven and that he hears and answers prayers. I accepted your word and believed it without question. I now

clearly recall an evening in the spring of 1949 when I was in
the sixth grade when this faith you had taught me became
more than just a belief.

You and Dad had just purchased a new pair of shoes for
me. As I remember, my old ones were so worn that we didn't
even bring them home from the store. I had just discovered
baseball and I wanted more than anything to play on the
school team, which I did. The night before we were to play
the 4th grade.

I was out in the apple orchard playing and running with
our dog, Lassie. It wasn't until you called me in that I noticed
the heel from my right shoe was missing. It wasn't the regular kind of heel, but one with deep tread. I knew that time
and money wouldn't permit a new one before school and the
game the next day. I must have spent an hour in that large
field looking in the grass for the heel. It was the needle in the
haystack. To an adult now this doesn't seem too serious but
to a young 12-year-old boy, nothing could have been more
serious.

Not able to find the heel on my own, I remembered your
teachings and knelt behind Grandma's house and told the
Lord of my problem and asked for a little help. When I got up
off my knees, it was almost dark and hard to find anything in
the grass even if you knew where it was. But you had told me
that He would hear and answer my prayers, so I walked back
out into the middle of the field. I closed my eyes and turned
around several times, telling the Lord that he had to take me
in the right direction. I stopped, opened my eyes and started
walking in the direction I was facing, with my eyes directed
at my feet as I walked. I had gone about half a block when my
foot stepped on the heel. There are those who might say that
was luck but I know different. You can imagine the joy in my
young heart at not only finding the lost heel, but knowing
that the Lord really lived and did listen to a young boy's
prayers.

Now if the Lord will listen and answer a young boy's
prayer about something as simple as a lost heel, I KNOW that
He will listen to the many, many prayers and days of fasting

of all those who know and love you. My mother's good health is a heck of a lot more important than a young boy's heel. YOU WILL BE OK!

A person is only given one real mother. You have always been a sweet, loving and understanding mother and I am thankful that you picked me to be your son. I love you so much and between fasting and prayer and taking up so much of the Lord's time He won't be able to do anything but grant us our prayers.

Mother, be at peace and rest assured that all will be well and that your family lives and needs you, Your loving son.

Needless to say, the Lord did hear and answer that man's prayer, just as he did the little boy's prayer.

Plane Crash

It was December, 1965, and we had just won our basketball game. I was riding high on a cloud as I waltzed in our front door. Thirty minutes later, I hit a low such as I had never experienced. The telephone had rung and I had answered with a happy hello. It was my brother—my eighteen year-old college freshman sister and her boyfriend were missing in his twin-engine Cessna plane.

The next three hours, we were all in a state of panic and shock as we prepared for the three-hour trip to Mesa. No more news came and we loaded the car. Just before we left, I went to my room, closed the door, and fell to my knees. I prayed at that time as I have never prayed before—words and promises came tumbling out. As I got off my knees, I was filled with a warm glow and a knowledge that my sister was okay.

The next three days went by in a sort of fog. I tried comforting my mother, my father, and the rest of the family as the Civil Air Patrol carefully searched for the plane. Wonderful friends and neighbors of my brother's came with food, volunteered to search, and gave words of comfort. All through the ordeal, I was sustained by my knowledge that my sister was okay. On the third day, my sister's Institute bishop brought the news that my sister and her boyfriend had been found—they had both been killed instantly as their small plane crashed into the mountain. The first thing that came to my mind and heart was a great flood of bitterness. The Lord had betrayed me. But as the first hurt wore off, I knew with a conviction that could not be shaken that the Lord had indeed given me the correct information.

My sister was in a far better place than this earth. She was now in a position to fulfill a far greater mission. I thanked my Heavenly Father for the joy she had brought into our lives and for the glorious plan of salvation that guaranteed me the right to see my sister again if I lived righteously. This one principle of the gospel was very forcibly and even joyfully imprinted in my mind and heart.

They Trotted Into the Corral

In the summer of 1959, I was herding about fifty head of Holstein cows for my Dad. I had been raised on this dairy farm of my father's, so I was fairly well-trained although only eight years of age. The Robert's canal cut our farm in half and it was my duty to keep the cattle on the grassy banks and out of the alfalfa fields that bordered the canal.

In the spring and early summer, the job added to the lazy, slow, pace of the warm weather because the cows were always full and content on the banks. As the summer grew older, it would grow hotter and drier and the cows became discontent. Their discontent had been building up for days and finally the lead cow, Bell (sometimes affectionately known as "Pig"), began being dumb like a fox and grazed to the edge of the field. I ran to get in front of her and she did not think much of the maneuver so she broke into a wild run and stampeded the whole herd. They all headed into the hay so I just ran after them. But the herd split up and stopped running to eat. I would drive one bunch toward the canal and then go after another only to have the last group come back. I began to panic because I had seen many cows bloat and die because they were found too late. I was as tired from running as an eight-year-old boy could be.

I was about to run to the house when the thought "pray for help" struck my mind. I fell to my knees in the thick alfalfa and prayed with all the might I could muster. As I jumped to my feet, I saw a miracle that would have made Moses blink even after the Red Sea. "Pig" was wolfing hay as fast as a New Holland baler when all at once her head went straight in the air and she let out a wild bellow, similar to a bull elephant, then stuck her feet in high gear and her tail straight in the air and headed for a weed patch next to the corral. Every cow followed her. After a small conference in the weed patch, they trotted into the corral.

Blacky

One Saturday, we were out fixing our newspaper box across the road and I was bringing a screwdriver to my dad. Then, our dog Blacky followed me to the road. We told her to go home. She turned around and walked away from the road. When I started to go across the road, Blacky followed me. When I was on the other side, Blacky was just beginning to go on to the road. A pickup truck was coming down the road and ran over her pelvis. We took Blacky up by the house and the girls and I ran in and said some prayers. After a lot of calling, we finally got in touch with the vet. When we got Blacky to the vet, he kept her. We were driving through town after that and were planning to have an ice cream cone, but my dad said we could fast or have an ice cream cone. We all decided to fast and pray. We prayed, "thy will be done." Blacky walked as soon as she got home.

A Father's Blessing

One of the greatest joys in belonging to the Church came the day I held my baby son in my arms to give him a name and a blessing. Having served a mission for the Church, I had been provided opportunities to exercise the priesthood I held. But using it to bless my son seemed to overshadow all my previous experiences. Just knowing that the Lord would allow me to use his priesthood to bless one of his children just beginning the mortal phase of his existence made the occasion really special.

It also made me realize the responsibility I had in giving him a blessing that would be worthy of him. And while I had in mind some specific blessings I wanted to give, it was wonderful to feel the spirit help me to remember them and bring to mind others I hadn't even thought of. It was also wonderful to feel the support of the others in the circle and to know that the priesthood really is a power.

The Bicycle Accident

I was baptized at the age of eight and yet Church was the last thing that interested me. My friends were all non-members, and I would much rather stay and play with them instead of going to Primary, Sunday School, or any Church meetings. I was in the sixth grade when my life took a dramatic change.

I was in a severe bicycle accident and suffered many injuries–broken hand, fractured skull, and no skin left on the left side of my face. I lay unconscious for many days. I lay in the hospital for a month without making much progress and then one day I took a turn for the worse. I lost all control of my body functions and didn't recognize anyone.

My father is not a member of the Church and my mother, as a last resort, turned to the Church. Two elders arrived promptly to give me a blessing and to this day I still can remember the feeling that came over me as the power of the priesthood filled that room. I don't remember the words, but I do remember the warm and wonderful feeling that overcame me. After that, I progressed at a rapid rate. The doctor still refers to me as his miracle child.

What a testimony building experience this was for me and my family. I often look at the scars left on my hand and face and say a silent prayer to my Father in Heaven, for after this accident I have never wavered in the Church.

Moved By the Spirit

A real spiritual experience happened to me while I was in Korea on my mission. I was sick and in the hospital. The day that I started feeling better, I stayed up late and was reading the Pearl of Great Price. While I was reading it, I started to feel warm all over and it felt as if the room was getting warmer and brighter. I never saw an angel or anything but I know that the Spirit of the Lord was there. Even today I can feel the same when I am reading the scriptures and feel especially moved by the Spirit.

Our Baby

My husband is a wonderful man who honors his priesthood and helps me in every way. He has given me four beautiful children. One, a boy, we lost shortly after birth. He was our third child and the events that happened leading up to and shortly after his birth helped to strengthen my testimony and faith. For quite a few weeks before he was born, while I would be doing my work or reading or doing things around my home, I would have a feeling that I was being watched, or I would hear someone call my name. When I would look up, I would see the form of a person standing there. I never could tell if it was a man or a woman, but I could tell it was a human form like a white vapor. It would stand there for a few seconds, then disappear.

My children often asked me if I was frightened when this happened, but I never was. I always had a feeling of being protected, of being watched over so that no harm would or could come to me. This baby was due in September of 1957.

A few days before Memorial Day of that year, my husband and I were at the cemetery cleaning off the grave of his father who passed away when my husband was only five. The individual families took care of their own family plots at this time. We were getting the grave prepared for Memorial Day. All of a sudden while I was standing there resting from raking, a voice said, "Come September you will have a grave here." I was startled and my husband asked me what was the matter. I told him what I had heard. I thought he had heard it too, but he had not. We talked about it a few minutes then went back to our work. At this time I had no thought that it might be the baby.

A few days later I went to bed trying to carry the baby full term or as long as I could to give it a better chance. Up to this time, I had not had any trouble of any kind. I was in perfect health. Our baby was born July 6, 1957 and lived only a few minutes. He was perfectly formed in every way, but as the weeks went by, we decided the Lord must have wanted and needed him worse than we did. Late that night after he was born, I was lying in my bed when this same voice came to me and said, "Name your baby Lloyd and put his name in all of your records." The next morning the first thing my husband said to me when he came in was, "We are supposed to give our baby a name and enter it in our records." He had been talking to our bishop earlier that morning and our bishop had told him that we should do this. It was done.

Principles

The greatest joy I have experienced in the Church has been when I have been most fully living the principles I know to be correct. Our life-style has taken us from the army, to working, to military separations, to students. In each environment, we have been active members of the Church. However, in some settings our strivings for perfection have not been as intense as in others. When we are not consciously striving and working for improvement, we fall behind in any progress we have previously made. When we get behind in tithing, we have more conflicts. When we miss a family home evening, it is easy to miss a family prayer. If we miss Church meetings, our patience and selflessness are nonexistent. When we are on a low spiritual plane, the house is messy and we are irritable.

On the other hand, our greatest joy has come with living these same principles closely. Being involved and active in those activities we know to be uplifting uplifts us. And when various crises occur, they are met boldly with a sound attitude, inner confidence, and strength which are not present in weaker spiritual settings.

My greatest joy has been realizing my potential in being a patient, understanding mother, a loving wife, a concerned and helpful neighbor, a supportive friend, a good Mormon. I can find these virtues only when I am at peace with myself. Only by knowing that I am uplifting myself by closely living gospel principles am I free to concentrate on uplifting others. And, by following this natural chain of laws, I find my greatest joy.

Trials

My greatest joy has probably been derived from learning how much we grow and develop through the trials and tribulations that we go through in this life. When my husband was killed at Geneva Steel eleven years ago, I felt a closeness with the Lord that I have never known before. I realized then that if we will only let him, he will see us through any trials that we have, if we will use faith and obey his commandments. I have never questioned any burdens that have been given me because I know the Lord loves me.

My daughter and her husband had been in a very serious automobile accident just before my husband died, and I was caring for them and their five children and five of my own at the time. Soon after, two grandchildren died and a sister-in-law and her three children. Two months after my husband's death, I was injured in an accident and have had three back surgeries and been in neck and back braces the last ten years. The Lord has given me the courage to keep going and still enjoy life. I am now attending college and am very thankful for being one of the most fortunate people alive.

Coming Home

I was sitting on my sleeping bag just off the edge of the road—highway 17–one-half mile out of Shamokin, Pennsylvania. It was raining. I was cold, wet, hungry, and unhappy–six months on the road strung out on drugs, coming down with hepatitis, trying to hitchhike to nowhere.

I thought, "What am I doing here? How did I get here?" But it didn't matter. I was being hip and liberated and doing my own thing. It was a long way I had travelled through the normal middle-class LDS experiences, Eagle Scout, Duty to God, and a mission. I wasted years and was old and miserable.

I thought, "Once I was happy; once I knew joy. Where did it go?" When I was twelve years old, I was ordained a deacon. On that day I knelt in a patch of weeds behind the garage and covenanted with the Lord.

"Dear Father in Heaven, I want to be happy. I want an education. I want a family. I want security and prestige in my community. I want to work in the kingdom and I want to know thee. Father, if you bless me with these things, I will do all in my power to obey thee and learn more of what I should do to fulfill all righteousness."

And the Lord said, "All right."

"Where did it go ? How can I get it back?"

I was twenty-four years old and I returned home to Sacramento, California. It was fall. The wind was blowing leaves and cold air about me. I walked up a familiar sidewalk to my own front door of years earlier. Shamokin, Pennsylvania was several miles and months behind, but the feeling was current.

On Sunday afternoon, I was coming home sick, tired, and empty. I knocked. The door opened–warmth, light, and love streamed from within the doorway and from the eyes of my mother who greeted me.

"How are you? Where have you been? Are you hungry? You don't look so well. It's good to see you. Sit down, son. Sure you're not hungry? Dad, come here. Joseph's home. He's back." My mother loved me. My mother wanted me.

"Hello, son. My, but it's good to see you, my boy. Have you come far?" My father loved me. My father wanted me.

"Virginia, fix this boy something to eat. He looks half starved. Would you like to go to Church with us?"

How could I go to Church with my family? I looked horrible. My clothes were filthy and I was sick.

"Son, we don't care what you look like or what anyone else thinks you look like. You're my boy. I'm damn proud of you and you belong with your family if that's where you want to be!"

He meant it—every word of it. Tears were in his eyes and his voice choked, and I loved him more.

I couldn't go with them; I was too ill. That has to be

what hell is like to see your family off about the Lord's work and unable to go with them.

As my mother closed the door behind her, she asked again, "Sure you're not hungry?"

How could I tell her how hungry I was and how she was feeding that hunger, how her smile and love was a feast to my empty spirit, how the gospel light—the light of Christ—which filled my home also bathed my wounds and healed my thirst.

I was left alone to bask in this pure "joy," but there was one more home, one more father and mother and family.

I was twenty-four years old and it had been twelve years since I had knelt in the weed patch behind the garage.

"Father, it's me again—Joseph. It's been so very long and I apologize. I want to try again. I need my family and someday my own wife and children. Yes, and an education and prestige and security and a future. I want to help in the kingdom and to know thee father. Bless me with this and I will do all I am able to be obedient and learn more of what I should do to fulfill all righteousness."

And again Father said, "Welcome home, Son. It's been long and hard. It's good to talk again. All right."

I have felt joy many times in my life, in many ways and degrees, but they are always the same, because it's always like coming home.

Rebaptized

My brother was excommunicated from the Church several years ago because of something he did. Watching him suffer and be as low as he was was a very hard thing for me, especially trying to understand why this had to happen to him. The sorrow of knowing that his name was blotted off of the records was something else, and everyday the pain of knowing this haunted me.

But my brother worked at his problem and overcame it. He took the right route for repentance. It was a long, hard climb, but he made it. Last year he was rebaptized and the joy our family felt was indescribable.

Knowing that you can be forgiven is a great joy and comfort to me.

Worthiness

One day my father got up as usual on Sunday morning to attend his bishop's meeting and that was the last I saw of him all day—he even missed Sunday School and Sacrament Meeting—until just before I went to bed that night. When he came in the house, he gathered all six of us kids and my mother into the living room and I noticed tears in his eyes. He told us that he and the rest of the bishopric had been fasting and praying all day long to find an MIA teacher. They each went into separate rooms with a list of all the ward members. They would choose whom they thought would be a good teacher, pray about it, then meet and compare notes. All day this went on and they never agreed upon one person. "Finally," he said, 'I had to search to the depth of my soul and repent of all of my sins and really humble myself before the Lord, and make myself worthy of the position I hold and the answer I was seeking before I could ask any questions.

By the time he was finished talking and bearing his testimony, we were all in tears. It was then that I realized the Church depended upon the righteousness of its members and leaders—not one person or family being better than another. I also gained a testimony of personal revelation.

"You Have God"

One early summer evening, a group of seminary students gathered to celebrate the graduation that had taken place earlier that day. The day had been particularly trying for me, and transportation to the party looked nil. Somehow, I got there and found myself among the group that are usually known as trouble makers. During the course of the evening, I found that I had said something terribly offensive around one of the finest persons that I know.

Upon realizing the foolishness of what I had said, I gathered within myself the courage to do what must be done. Feeling that humility that one can only feel when asking for forgiveness, I told the person involved the incident as it had occurred. This person did not even know what had happened, which was one of my early fears. But, that person put her arms around me and told me that she

was glad I had come to her. I thanked her for her friendship and understanding and told her that I wish I had
more friends like her. Then she said one of the most
important things I have ever been told. She said, "You do,
you have God'"

How great was the feeling that burned in my soul.
How beautiful to know that God truly lives and is my
friend. And what great ecstasy to know one is forgiven
after going through the proper steps of repentance.

Service

In all of my many Church positions, I have especially
loved working with the youth. Assisting the young people
to develop their talents and potentials is truly a gratifying
experience. One young boy in particular always comes to
mind when I think of working with the youth. This
young man was a convert to the Church. His parents
were not members and were somewhat opposed to his
joining the Church. They offered no encouragement for
his Church activities, although they never stopped him
from attending meetings and functions. This young man
desired to serve a mission for the Lord, but had limited
financial means of support. Realizing full well that he
would have to carry the financial burden entirely by himself, he worked part time during the school year and full
time during the summer months to finance his mission.
It was my opportunity to assist this individual in preparing for his mission, both spiritually and financially. We
often took time just to sit and talk together about the

gospel. It was very important for him to have someone to talk to. Often we would go together to welfare projects and special youth firesides. It was a great experience for me just to "be there" when he needed advice and counsel, or just someone to discuss the gospel with. During the course of his mission, I assisted financially and received so much more in return than I ever was capable of giving.

This young man was able to serve an honorable and dedicated mission. His efforts in the mission field brought many individuals to a knowledge of the truth of the gospel. His greatest contribution, however, was his example to his parents. They began, slowly but surely, to see the importance of the gospel in this young man's life. Upon his return his parents were markedly more open-minded and willing to listen about the gospel.

Service and understanding go hand in hand. So many times members of the Church need someone to listen to their problems, discouragements, and set-backs. A person, truly in tune with the Spirit, can be of invaluable service to another by taking the time to serve them by listening with them, crying with them, and laughing with them. Service and concern for others are the things which have truly helped me to find true happiness in the gospel. For it is truly when we are in the service of our fellowmen that we are in the service of our God.

Lost Sheep

As it says in the Doctrine and Covenants 15:18, "How great shall be your joy if you bring save it be one soul into the Kingdom of God." I believe I have experienced this joy to a little degree. As a deacon and teacher, I was one of the group leaders who always tried to help the inactive boys. During this time, there was one boy who was always inactive and hard to reach. He had a bad home life, with his mom wanting a divorce from his dad. He was always working on Sunday for his dad. About the time I became a priest, he suddenly realized the gospel was important to him, and he quit his job, made a complete turn-around, and is very active. Right now, he is the secretary in our priests quorum and is planning on a mission and doing a great job.

I was probably no help in bringing this lost sheep back, but I received joy from seeing his change and happiness. This is why I want to go on a mission and "bring back many souls unto the kingdom of God," and receive joy for it.

Helping Others

As a girl, I can remember my mother serving in the Relief Society. She was a counselor and helped in teaching, but what impressed me the most was how she helped the needy in welfare work. She would deliver food to the door of some needy family, knock and leave before they could see who brought it. She would gather clothes, tend sick children, straighten up some sick sister's home and prepare delicious meals. She would do this happily and never complained. I loved to go with her. I was happy, too, for I felt I was helping someone who really needed it.

My father helped on the welfare farm in Ohau, Hawaii. He always took us kids and we really did work hard. We cleared weeds and planted young papaya trees— and why? My father told us it would help feed needy families who couldn't afford food. To think that we as young children could actually help someone was wonderful. It made us work even harder.

I love the Church for it gives members a reason to live. To give service to others makes one forget one's self and one's own problems. One then sees that he/she really isn't that bad off but has many wonderful blessings.

"Who Would Do Something Like This?"

A seminary teacher, a very intimate and dear friend of mine, had been sick and out of work for a few months. He and his small family lived in a small apartment. The cupboards and rooms were as barren as a field mouse's den. It was obvious to me that their Christmas was going to prove just as barren.

It was only the next day that our old group of high school friends got together and determined to take welfare into our own hands. We scraped together what little money we could and systematically divided the responsibilities among ourselves. Our group selflessly spent the next week playing Santa Claus to someone who might never know. Strangely, that made our gift all the more rewarding to give. And I shall never forget the amazed joy on the family's faces as I returned with them from an evening drive to find a decorated tree in the living room, the floor filled with presents, and the cupboards restocked with food. Above all else the peaceful, unassuming reward which most inspired me was to hear them say to themselves, "Who would do something like this...for us?"

It was then, at seventeen, that I first realized that Christmas is much more than something for me. For no greater joy or sweeter peace has filled me then or since than that which accompanied one singular act of service.

Bishop Peterson's Yard

One of the experiences that has brought me joy in the Church is when my dad and I volunteered to go work in Bishop Peterson's yard. I had a great feeling working side by side with a General Authority. It made me feel good because he didn't treat me like I was little. I wish that I could have another opportunity like that sometime again.

Prayer Works

In our Sunday School class we have a boy that is on drugs and smokes. He hasn't been to Church for two years. So our teacher told us to all say "hi" for one week. So on Sunday, we came back and we told our teacher that he had been friendlier. The next week our teacher told us to ask him to Church. Our class went home and we prayed that we might be friends with him and he would come. We did this for one month. The next week he came and all of us were happy and it strengthened my testimony that prayer works.

On the Road to Recovery

The thing that brings me the most joy is people who give blessings in our Church. We were playing and my friend pushed me off and I fell off the top of a bunk bed. I fell on my head on a cement floor. My head swelled and I couldn't see right. After that, I couldn't remember very much except that I was taken to the hospital and the doctors took pictures and told me to lay still. When I came home, my dad and a neighbor put some oil on my head. I laid still for the blessing and asked Heavenly Father to help me get better. I was still very sick but after a few days I was feeling much better. When this happened, I was four years old and was living in Salt Lake.

(Kent had a fractured skull, and it was feared he would not live, but after the blessing his condition almost reversed and he was on the road to recovery.)

Tammy

On the night of October 2, 1974, one of my very good friends was killed in a car-train accident. The train hit her side of the car and she was instantly killed. The rest of her family lived. Her dad had been a bishop and they were one of the closest Mormon families that I have known.

I have an everlasting love for Tammy and I'll always remember her sweet spirit. If it wasn't for the fact of our plan of salvation I could and would never accept her death for she was a great example and joy in my life. This was the first flower that had ever wilted in my garden and it was very, very hard for me to accept it. But I know that she is delighted to see her Heavenly Father and his son, Jesus Christ, whom she loved more than anyone. Because I love her, I want to try to my fullest to reach the Celestial Kingdom so I can share our love and friendship again for I am a Child of God!

Listening to Promptings

An experience my sister Mary had last year is most impressive. She surely listens to the promptings of the Spirit. As a family we have always said she has a sixth sense.

Driving from school to home one day on the San Diego Freeway, she says a voice that seemed to be from someone sitting beside her said, "Mary, something is wrong with your car." She drove to the first service station she could find and when they asked her what was the matter, she said, "It just does not act right." The men pronounced the car fine. She drove away and again the voice said, "Mary, something is wrong with your car." Again she went to a station and was told the car was in fine shape. The third time the same thing happened. She drove to the station and was told all things were in splendid condition. She started up the engine and as she started to drive away from the garage, the steering wheel fell in her lap.

Sealed

It was my first time in the temple–except when I was very young and I did some baptisms. My sister and I waited in the nursery with my six-month-old nephew. We were nervous and excited with anticipation. But we were calmed by the peace and gentleness there. We were taken up to the sealing room. We sat with our parents while the Stake President explained what we were to do. I've never seen my parents so beautiful and happy and I've never felt such rich, warm joy inside me as I felt when we all knelt around the alter. We clasped hands and the Stake President said, "Hold on, because I'm going to seal you real tight."

The joy of knowing I'd be with those wonderful people in the presence of our Savior and Father in Heaven was more than I can ever express. I felt like my insides would glow right through my skin with all my happiness.

The Lord Knows

I came to study at BYU in spite of my dislike for the United States and in spite of the reputation that BYU has

as a "marriage institution." When I arrived here, I had so
many bad experiences that I always wondered why. Why
had the Spirit told me to come here?

Last May I knew the answer. My parents called me
early in the morning from Argentina and they told me my
father had been set apart as a patriarch of a newly organized stake and that they were coming in October for the
general conference of the church and that we were going
to be able to go through the temple.

Last October, for the first time, I received my endowments and was sealed to my parents, just like my patriarchal said. What a joyful experience. I had never thought
this blessing would be fulfilled so soon and would bring
such a joy to my life. It was my best spiritual experience,
and it was then that I knew why I was here, even though I
still did not like to be in this country. I learned that the
"Lord knows" why we are supposed to do things and that
we are supposed to obey the promptings of the Spirit even
when we do not like what He says to us. I will always
thank him to have had the chance of listening to the
answer of a prayer to decide to come here.

A Mother's Prayer

I am grateful I can talk through prayer to my Heavenly
Father and that He answers many of my prayers in my
behalf. For example, when I found out I could only have
three children, I prayed to Heavenly Father and asked him
if I could help other people raise their children. I have had

many opportunities to work in primary, mutual, and taught early morning seminary for four years. The last five years since my husband died, I have been a head resident on campus to 242 girls each year and many young people during the summer. Helping other people improve their lives has brought much joy to my life.

Pray

One morning I awoke feeling troubled and had great difficulty getting through the usual tasks of a wife and mother. As the morning progressed, feelings of despair, dark depression, fear and finally terror came over me and I knew that something evil was trying to overpower me. I dared not look over my shoulder for fear of what I would see. The presence of evil was so strong. I could not think clearly and was very confused and frightened. Finally something prompted me to call my husband at work. I was very upset and could not keep from crying when I told him what was happening to me and that I couldn't think what to do. Then—bless him—he very calmly gave me the simple but profound answer. "Pray. Go and pray, and call me back as soon as you can." I locked myself in the bathroom and knelt and cried as I tried to pray. Finally, I was able to ask my Father to help me. As I knelt, sobbing, I felt as if someone put hands upon my head and blessed me. A great peace came over me. I knew the Lord was near and would give me strength.

Through this and other experiences during my life, he has borne witness to me that He loves me, and this knowledge gives me a deep peace and sense of security, and abiding sense of well-being—which is one definition of happiness.

The Deacon's Quorum President

Probably the greatest joy is the knowledge that Christ lives and that we have provided for us a way to return back to our Heavenly Father and live with Him. I find great joy in reading and studying about the gospel. I find great joy in serving the youth and watching them grow.

An experience comes to mind when we were trying to come up with a name for a Deacon's quorum president. The name that the Spirit dictated to us was a boy with family problems, long hair, a bad attitude, and always against any leadership. But we submitted the name to the bishop and asked that he pray with us on behalf of that name.

A week later we asked about the boy and the bishopric agreed with us, but asked about the hair and dress standards. It was decided that we would not approach the boy about cutting his hair, but explain to him his responsibility. The week following, when he was to be sustained, he came to priesthood meeting well-groomed and his hair cut. He has become very strong in the Church and a great leader.

There are many experiences of success with the youth and their willingness to serve. This brings great joy to me to see their willingness and their testimonies grow.

The Interview

We were part of a group of Explorer scouts and leaders camped near Governor's Lake in the Uinta Mountains of northern Utah. My calling in the Church at that time was bishop. Inviting my son, Jim, to join me on a short hike, I soon found a quiet, beautiful opening in the pines where we sat together on a fallen log. In this setting we talked about the Priesthood of God, our worthiness and willingness to serve him and the importance of living so we could feel free and worthy to accept any blessing or call to service which may come. This was a special moment for each of us. As a father, I was happy and grateful for a son who was honoring his home and parents. As a bishop I was happy for a young member of the Aaronic Priesthood who was completely worthy to be recommended for ordination to the office of priest. Jim didn't know he was being interviewed by his bishop for this purpose. It was one of the most meaningful interviews which I ever held.